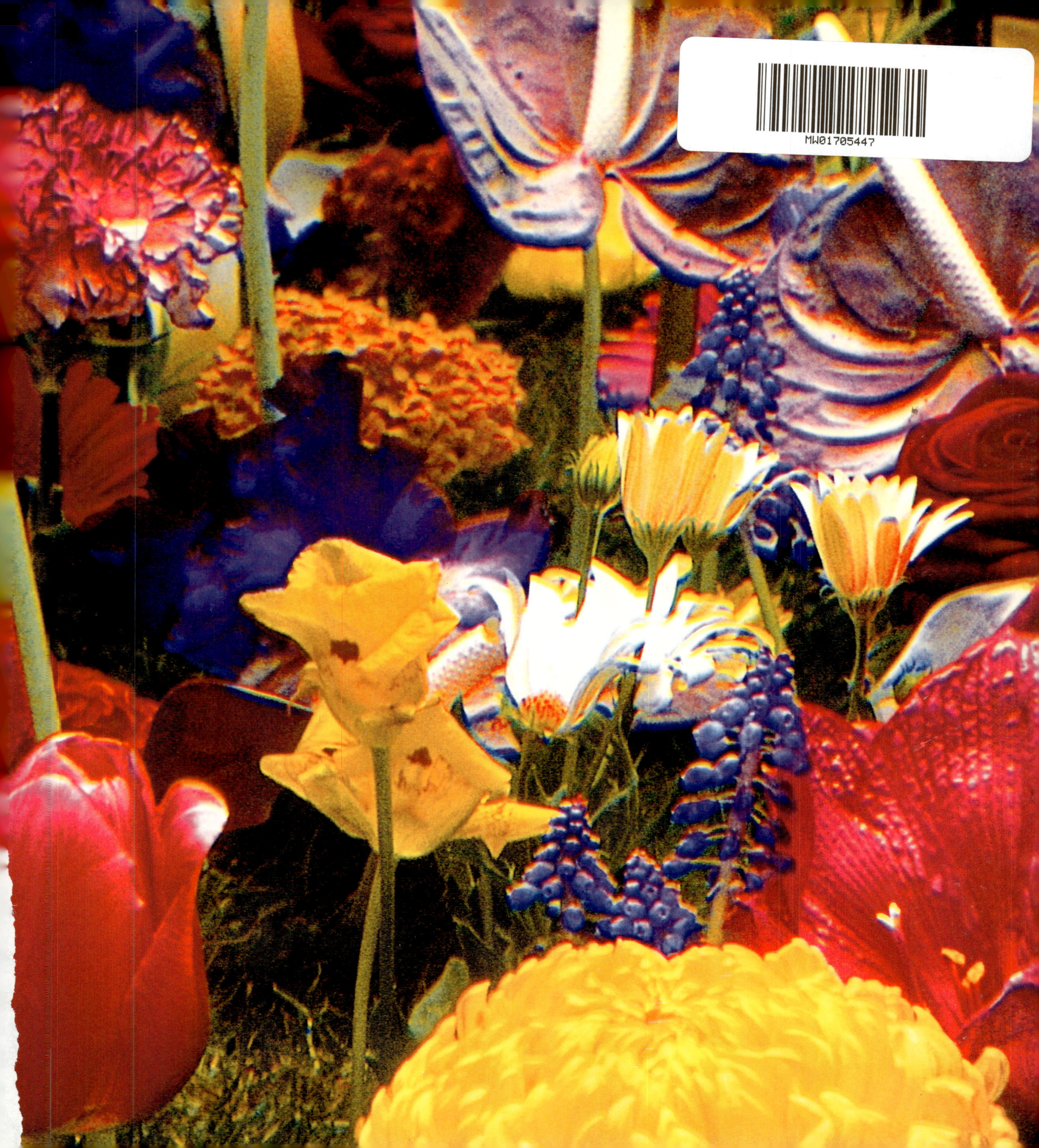

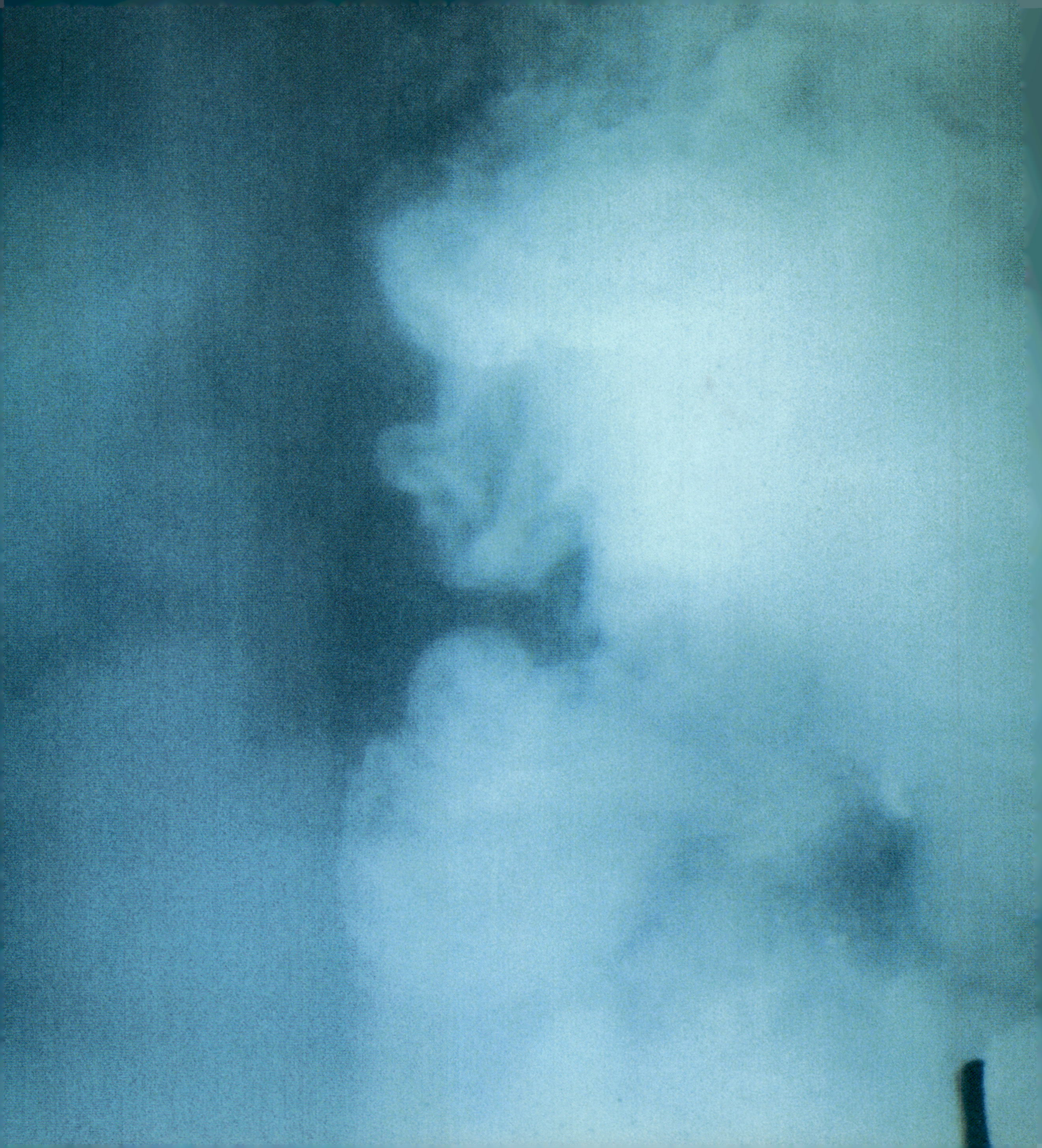

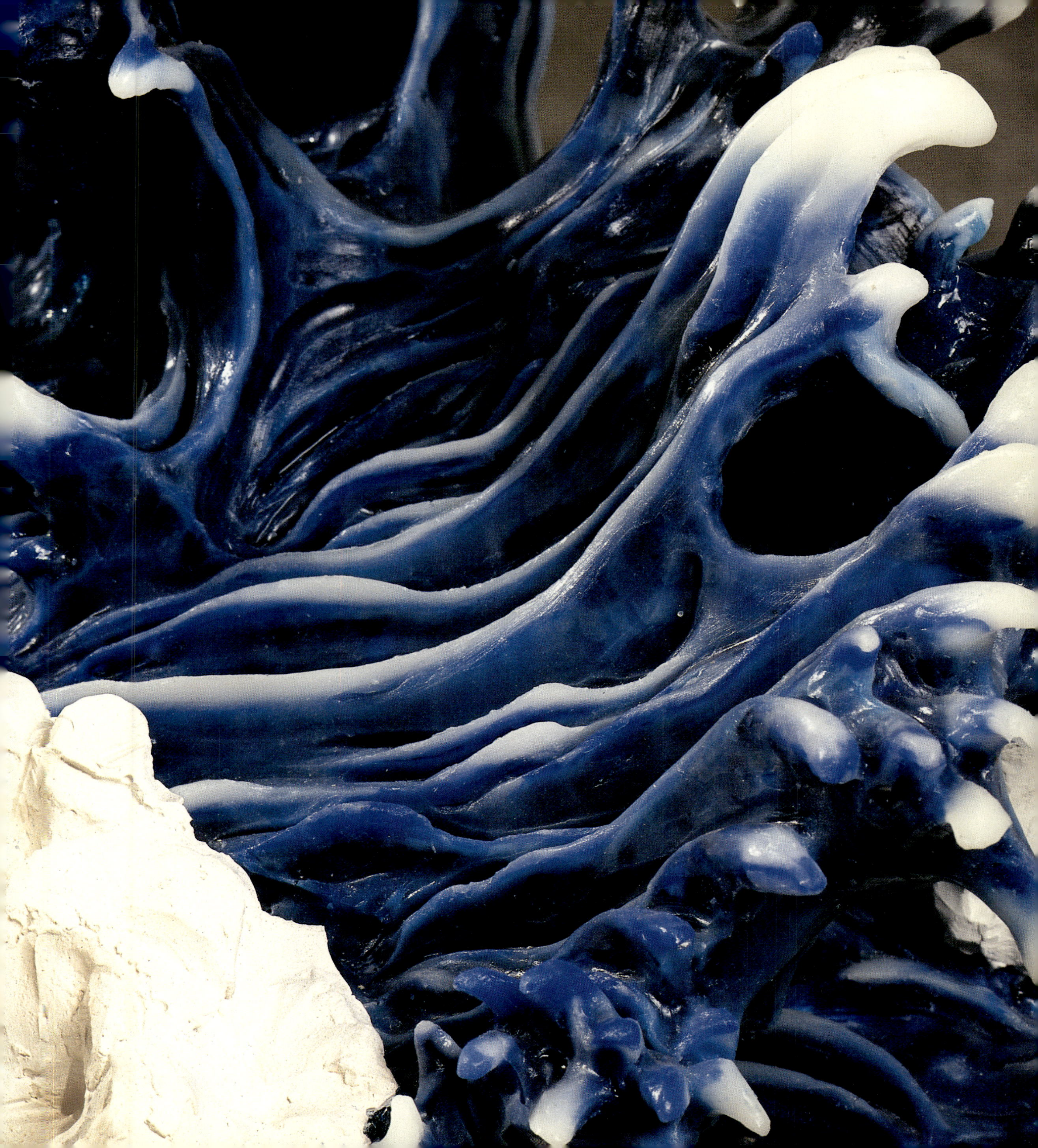

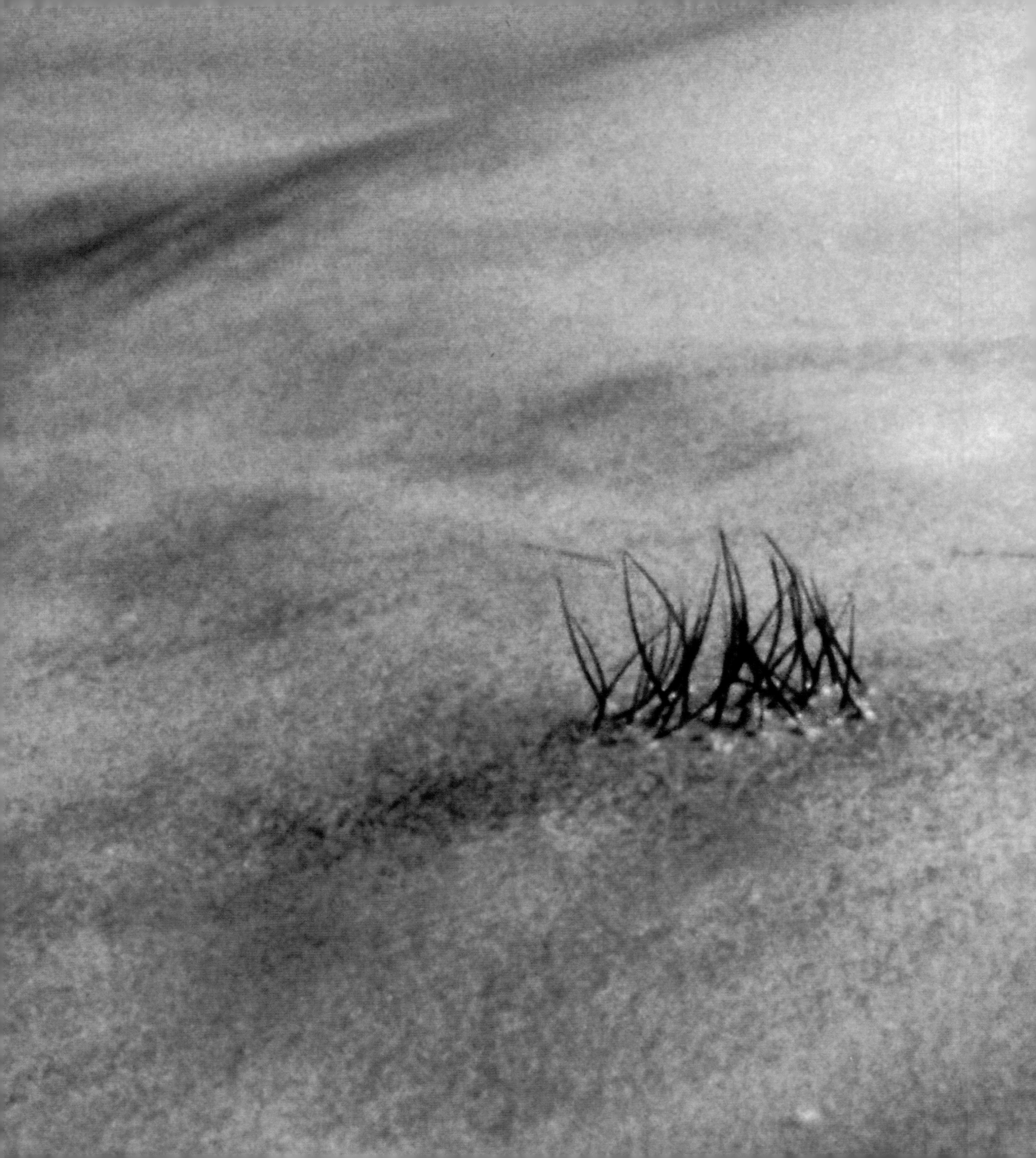

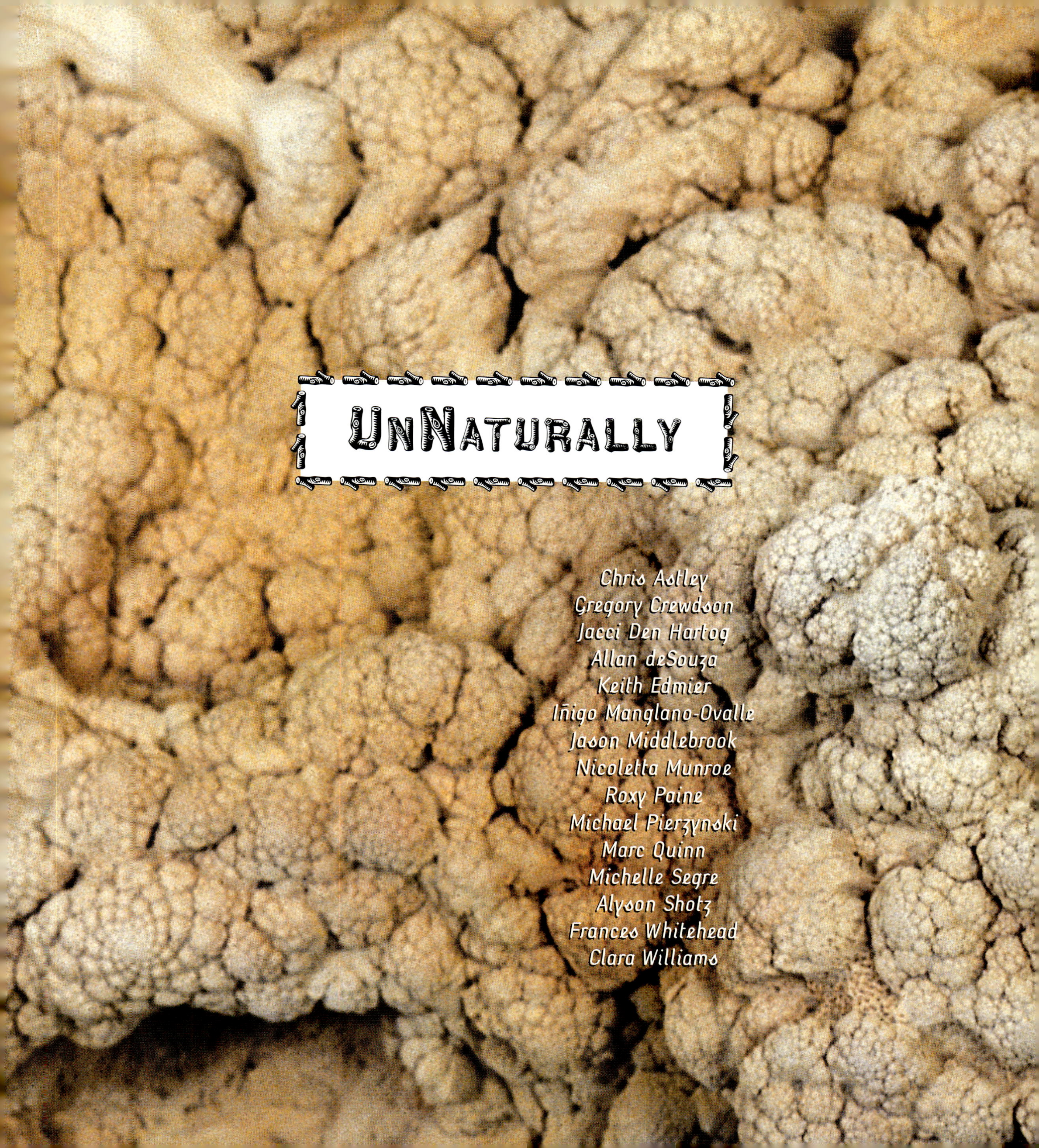

# UnNaturally

Chris Astley
Gregory Crewdson
Jacci Den Hartog
Allan deSouza
Keith Edmier
Iñigo Manglano-Ovalle
Jason Middlebrook
Nicoletta Munroe
Roxy Paine
Michael Pierzynski
Marc Quinn
Michelle Segre
Alyson Shotz
Frances Whitehead
Clara Williams

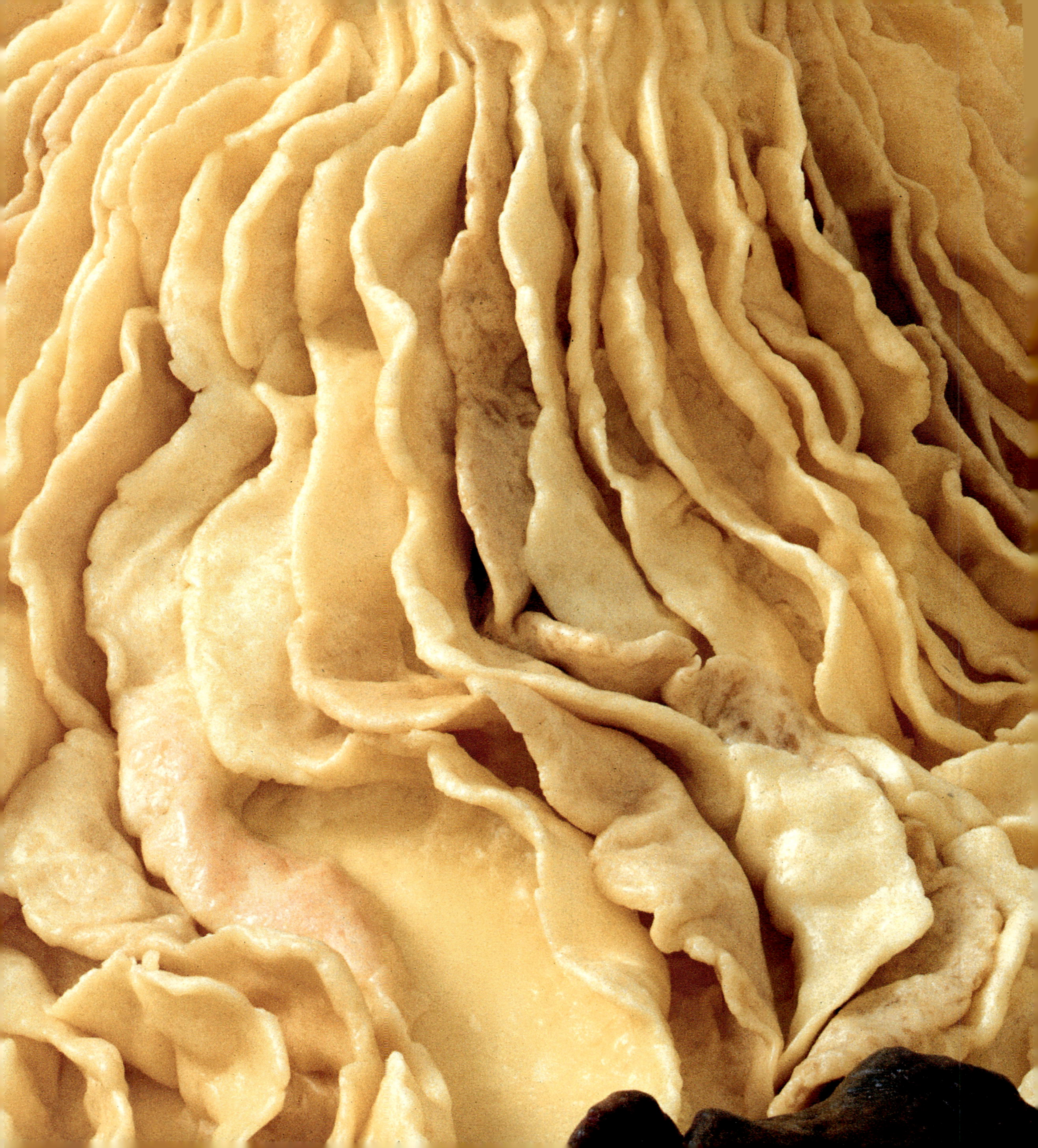

Essay by curator
Mary-Kay Lombino

# UnNaturally

With a short story by
Philip K. Dick

Independent Curators International
New York

Published to accompany the traveling exhibition *UnNaturally*, organized and circulated by Independent Curators International (ICI), New York

Exhibition curated by Mary-Kay Lombino

EXHIBITION FUNDER
Elizabeth Firestone Graham Foundation

PHOTO CREDITS
Page 1
MARK QUINN
*Garden*[2], 2000 (detail)

Page 2
JACI DEN HARTOG
*Garden for Walking Through Water*, 1999 (detail)

Page 3
CHRIS ASTELY
*Volume VI*, 2000 (detail)

Page 4
ALLAN DESOUZA
*Terrain #7*, 1999–2000 (detail)

Page 5
ROXY PAINE
*Tapioca Slime Painting*, 2000 (detail)

Page 6
MICHELLE SEGRE
*Untitled*, 2000 (detail)

EXHIBITION ITINERARY*

Contemporary Art Museum
University of South Florida
Tampa, Florida
January 13–March 8, 2003

H & R Block Artspace at the
Kansas City Art Institute
Kansas City, Missouri
September 19–October 29, 2003

Fisher Gallery
University of Southern California
Los Angeles, California
November 21, 2003–January 17, 2004

F. Donald Kenney Museum
The Regina A. Quick Center for the Arts
St. Bonaventure University
St. Bonaventure, New York
February 3–March 30, 2004

Copia: The American Center for Wine, Food & the Arts
Napa, California
April 20–August 16, 2004

Lowe Art Museum
University of Miami
Coral Gables, Florida
September 14–November 14, 2004

**at time of publication*


799 Broadway, Suite 205
New York, NY 10003
Tel: 212-254-8200 Fax: 212-477-4781
www.ici-exhibitions.org



Library of Congress Catalog Number: 2002114435
ISBN: 0-916365-66-2
Editor: Stephen Robert Frankel
Designer: Amanda S. Washburn
Printed in Germany by Cantz

## *Table of Contents*

## *Lenders to the Exhibition*

Chris Astley
Ruth and Jake Bloom
Jacci Den Hartog
Allan deSouza
Michael Formica and Bob Heimstra
Lisa and Stuart Ginsberg
Nicole Klagsbrun Gallery, New York
Iñigo Manglano-Ovalle
Jason Middlebrook
Nicoletta Munroe
Roxy Paine
Patrick Painter, Santa Monica, California
Friedrich Petzel Gallery, New York
Michael Pierzynski
Marc Quinn
Lawrence Rickels
Michelle Segre
Alyson Shotz
Frances Whitehead

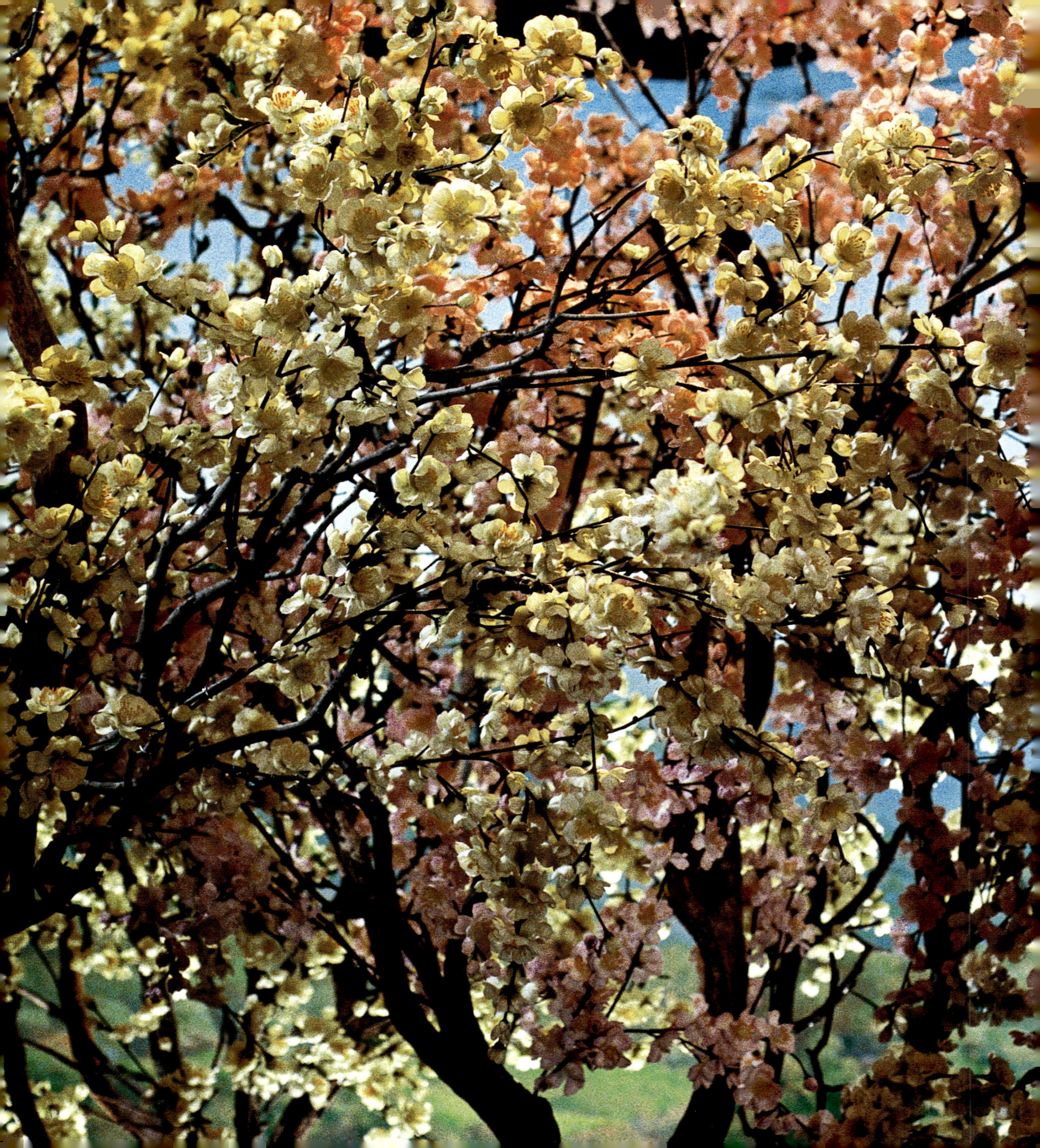

## *Foreword and Acknowledgments*

Independent Curators International is dedicated to enhancing the understanding and appreciation of contemporary art through traveling exhibitions that give viewers across the country and abroad the opportunity to see and experience important recent developments in art internationally. *UnNaturally* presents a visually intriguing and conceptually thought-provoking selection of works by artists from across the country and abroad who are asking us to consider our changing experience of nature. This compelling and timely topic is currently being explored not only by visual artists but also by writers, filmmakers, and others who sense a quiet revolution taking place.

Mary-Kay Lombino, the curator of *UnNaturally*, aptly begins her essay here with a quote by Charles Darwin from 1859, while the short story by Philip K. Dick reprinted here is set in the distant future in a place beyond our solar system. Today, we are well aware of the complex and often conflicting relationship that has developed between nature and culture. We see ourselves as citizens of the planet Earth, concerned about the fragility of the natural environment in our own communities and around the globe, about whole ecosystems endangered, extinctions threatened, and species destroyed. At the same time, while we work to save nature, we are surrounded by newly invented forms of nature meant to improve our lives (such as healthier plants packed with more nutrients) or to bring the out-of-reach serenity and enjoyment of the natural world to urbanites (in theme parks, malls, and zoos). An ambiguity has developed between what we consider to be real or artificial, along with a debate about which is superior. At the same time, the life-enhancing qualities we see in nature makes it second only to sex as a merchandizing lure.

An intense debate surrounds the complex and sometimes conflicting issues involved in saving the planet while improving human life, advancing culture, and preserving long-held values. The artists in *UnNaturally* address all of these, but focus especially on our relationship with man-made nature and the differences between real and imitation, inspired and provoked by the amusing, alluring, and disturbing experiences of "nature" we encounter each day.

18.
NICOLETTA MUNROE
*Cherry Blossoms II*
*(Stage Center)*, 2000 (detail)

This traveling exhibition and catalogue have been made possible through the encouragement, dedication, and generosity of many people. First and foremost, on behalf of ICI's Board of Trustees and staff, I extend our sincere thanks and appreciation to Mary-Kay Lombino. With her broad knowledge of contemporary art practices, she defined and developed this timely and provocative exhibition, and has, through her thoughtful catalogue essay, given us insight into the works included in the exhibition and the artists who created them.

We are proud to present *UnNaturally*, and wish to express special thanks to all the artists. Their involvement and support have been crucial to the success of this project. We also want to convey special thanks to Jason Middlebrook, Roxy Paine, and Frances Whitehead for creating new works for the exhibition.

All of us at ICI convey our sincere thanks to the Elizabeth Firestone Graham Foundation for its support of the exhibition.

ICI owes a tremendous debt of gratitude to all the lenders who generously allowed their works to travel throughout the two-year tour and to the many galleries for their assistance.

I am very pleased to extend special thanks from Mary-Kay to Rebecca Andersson for her skillful curatorial assistance. Ms. Lombino is also thankful to Ralph Rugoff for sharing his knowledge and guidance, to Jane Hart for her contagious enthusiasm for the project, and to Eric Steinman for his moral support and insightful feedback.

Sincere appreciation is due to Amanda S. Washburn for her design of this catalogue, and to Stephen Robert Frankel, editor. It was a great pleasure to work with both of these superb professionals. I would also like to recognize Paul Di Filippo who guided us to Philip K. Dick's wonderful story.

ICI's dedicated, knowledgeable, and enthusiastic staff deserves recognition for their efforts on this project. Thanks go especially to Carin Kuoni, director of exhibitions, Carolyn Padwa Temlock, registrar, and Amy Owen, exhibitions assistant, who worked on every aspect of this exhibition and publication. Thanks also to Nika Elder, exhibitions assistant, and to Sarah Andress, our former exhibitions assistant; Hedy Roma, director of development; Eileen Choi, development associate; Sue Scott, executive assistant and press coordinator; exhibitions intern Gabe Herman; and Dolf Jablonski, bookkeeper. 

Finally, I extend my warmest appreciation to ICI's Board of Trustees for their continuing support and commitment to all of ICI's activities. They join me in expressing our gratitude to everyone who has contributed to making this project possible.

Judith Olch Richards
*Executive Director*

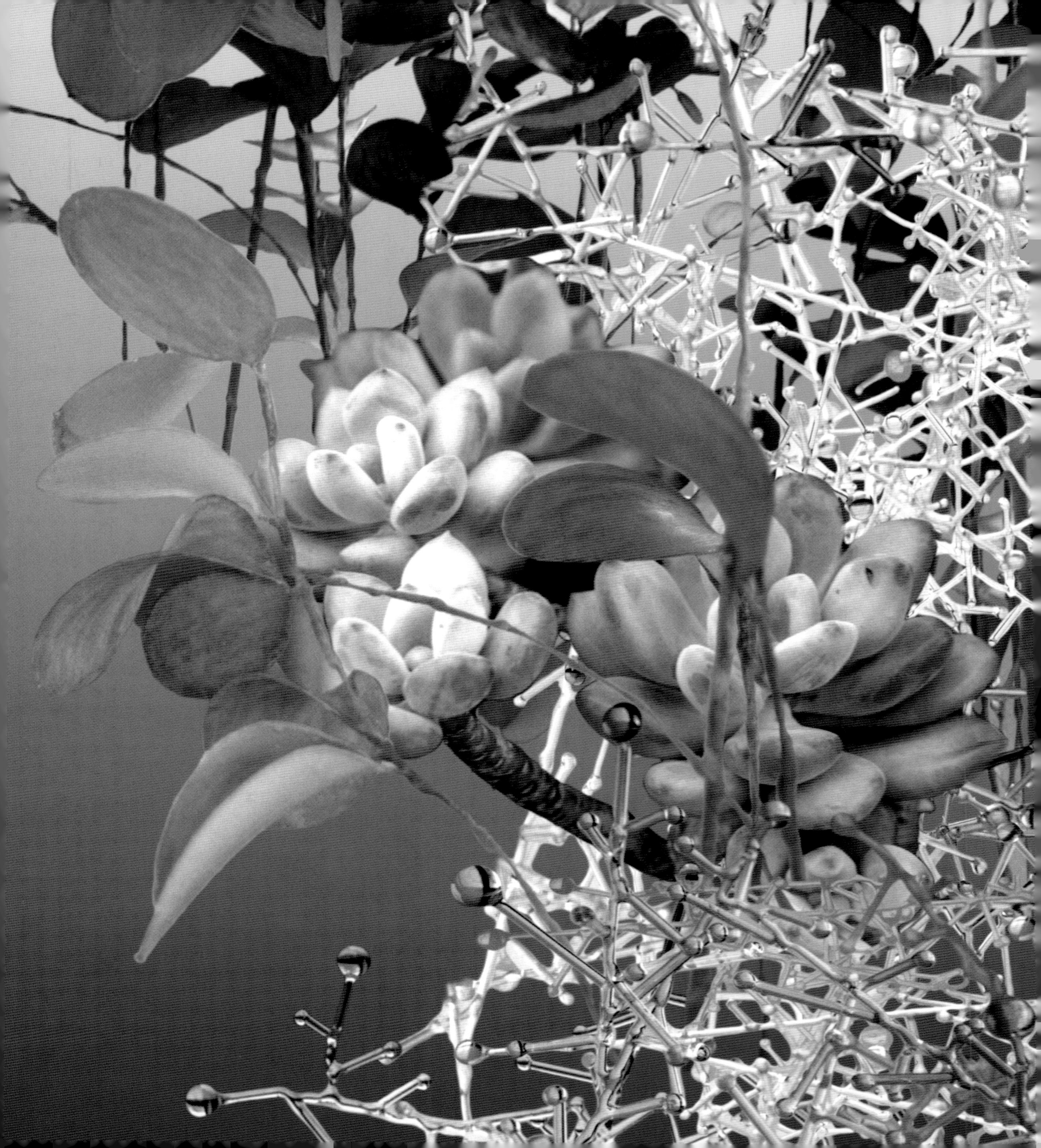

*Mary-Kay Lombino*

# Artists in the Garden

## WHERE NATURE AND CULTURE COLLIDE

*How fleeting are the wishes and efforts of man!*
*How short his time! And consequently how poor his products*
*will be, compared with those accumulated by nature*
*during whole geological periods. Can we wonder, then,*
*that nature's productions should be far "truer"*
*in character than man's productions; that they should be*
*infinitely better adapted to the most complex*
*conditions of life, and should plainly bear the stamp of far*
*higher workmanship?*[1] —Charles Darwin, 1859

Although Charles Darwin's view of the natural world, regarded as radical in his time, is now widely accepted, cultural critics today undoubtedly judge his criteria for "trueness" and "workmanship" as outdated. Since Darwin's time, the rapid and continual rise of industrialization and urbanization has permanently changed the relationship between humans and the environment in which we live, which has evolved into a complex dichotomy of culture versus nature that even Darwin could not have predicted. These days, we are beginning to see a collapsing of the two categories. As our environment becomes more and more man-made, it is hardly possible to maintain the belief that nature and culture can still be considered mutually exclusive. In this age of biomimicry, in which most living matter—including human embryos—can be bred in a Petri dish, can "nature's productions" any longer be considered superior to "man's productions"? Modern technology has by now blurred the boundaries between natural and artificial. One might question whether nature that has been manipulated by man could still be considered nature. Or perhaps, at this point in history, nature is entirely a cultural construction. Should we view nature as simply another category of culture?

1. *Charles Darwin,* ON THE ORIGIN OF SPECIES *[facsimile of the first edition] (Cambridge, Mass.: Harvard University Press, 1964; original publ. 1859), p. 84.*

32.
ALYSON SHOTZ
*False Branches #5*, 2001 (detail)

Are we more interested in a dialogue with nature, or in dominating it to fulfill our own needs?

In line with a long tradition of looking to nature for inspiration, many in a new generation of artists are intrigued by these issues and address them in their work. I invite the viewers of *UnNaturally* to explore the differences that still remain between real nature and imitation nature through the work of sixteen artists who simulate nature through "artificial" means. These artists examine how our experience of reality is affected by human intervention into the natural order of things and the role that socially constructed notions of nature play in this equation; and they pique our desire both to keep the categories of culture and nature separate and to embrace technological advances that increase our ability to replicate our environment. The works in the exhibition reflect the artificiality that surrounds us today in a world that has been reshaped and rearranged to fit with our idealized notions of nature.

## NATURE FOR SALE

Nature has long carried the powerful myth of a once-intrinsic and now-unattainable authenticity and purity, epitomized by the story of Adam and Eve's expulsion from the Garden of Eden. We consider nature to be at once the wild, untamed outdoors; a solitary refuge from the city; a destination for adventure; and a utopian reality outside us that elicits a variety of emotions. "The natural world" has become a catch phrase that means all these different things, each of which represents an authentic experience that we desire. Modern-day anxiety over dwindling ecological resources has heightened our desire to coexist in harmony with our planet, yet the impact of technology continues to eat away at the natural environment and, in turn, at our collective conscience. Nevertheless, experiences of real nature are valuable commodities that we must work for, and often pay for.

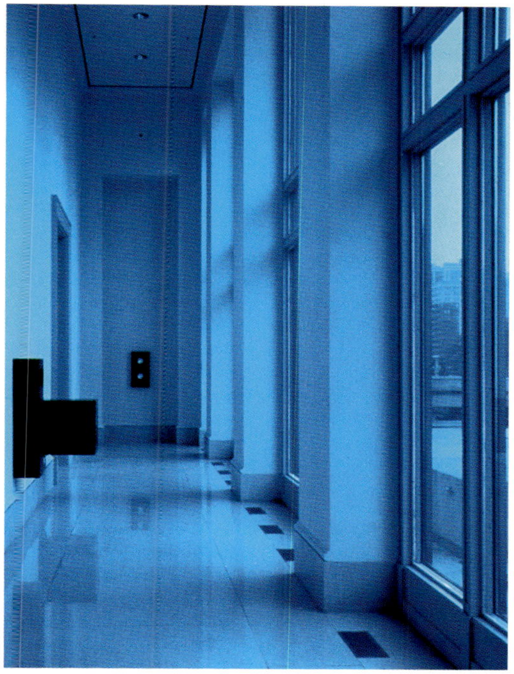

16.
IÑIGO MANGLANO-OVALLE
*Sonambulo II*, 1999
installation (southern view),
Art Institute of Chicago
(This work, originally created as
a sound-and-light installation,
is presented in this exhibition
as a sound installation.)

As soon as anything, especially something as vague as nature, becomes commodified, our understanding of it is mediated by the way it is packaged, marketed, and sold. In our consumer-driven society, culture is dominated by the influence of the corporate mentality more than ever before. Nothing is safe from commodification: our actions, our beliefs, and our purchases are studied by market analysts in order to evaluate what we might be likely to spend our money on—be it an outdoor adventure that simulates being in the wild, an S.U.V. that can take us off-roading into the backcountry, or artificial versions of nature in the form of packaged goods.

Such co-opting and merchandizing of nature's allure is examined in the work of several artists in the exhibition. Iñigo Manglano-Ovalle, for example, scrutinizes the practice of buying canned sounds of nature on compact disc. For his sound installation *Sonambulo* (cat. no. 18)—the title is the Spanish word for sleepwalker—Manglano-Ovalle created an original track of ambient sound that imitates "New Age" C.D.'s featuring recorded rainstorms, waves breaking, and other sounds from nature. Such sound tracks are customized for and marketed to upper-middle-class urbanites to help them relax and tune out the stresses of the city. Ironically, Manglano-Ovalle's raw material is the clamorous sound of a gunshot he recorded in his neighborhood in Chicago. Using sophisticated technology in a recording studio, he "pixelated" the recorded shot into tiny segments of sound and transformed it into the calm, soothing, ambient noise of a rolling thunderstorm. In *Sonambulo*, Manglano-Ovalle makes an issue of our readiness to accept mere appearance as reality, fooling us into thinking that we're hearing the real thing—or at least a recording of it.

Michael Pierzynski's diminutive sculptures recall souvenir-shop trinkets that evoke an experience of a particular place. He often mimics mementos of the natural world, as when we bring home a seashell from the beach or an acorn from a walk in the woods, but taking the idea one step further by creating his own artificial mementos of nature. His three wall sculptures, one of which is shown here, *Untitled* (brown) (cat. no. 25), are ceramic replicas of

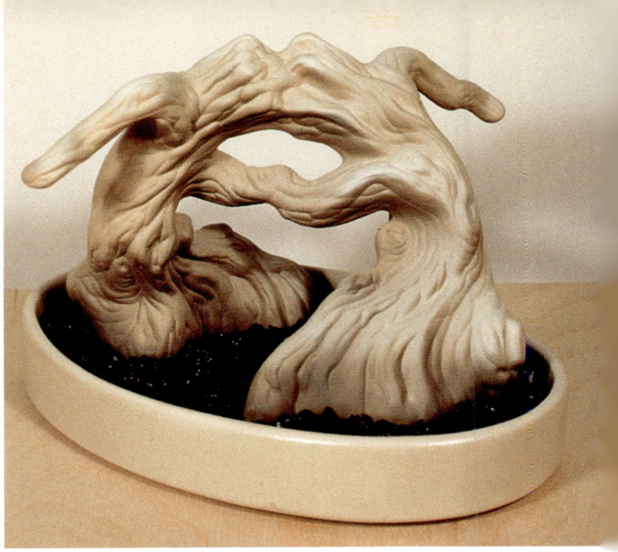



twin pairs of hedge apples—the fruit of the Osage orange tree, a species of mulberry that is native to the south-central region of the United States. This unpalatable fruit looks like a strange cross between an apple and an orange. Made from a single mold, each replica is identical in size, shape, and surface texture, with only their color—faux-natural shades of green and brown—distinguishing one from the others. In an ironic twist, the perfect uniformity of the fake fruits violates certain ideas of "naturalness" that we cling to, such as the idiosyncratic individuality of each "product" of nature. In these works, Pierzynski wryly comments on what it means to have a token from a particular place in an age of globalization, where difference among cultures has eroded and conformity has spread across borders and oceans.

Pierzynski's *Cultivating Internal Plastic Infinity* (cat. no. 24), presents an even more pointed commentary on the practice of merchandizing nature's wonders. Here, he presents a memento of the natural world as a typical product of kitsch culture. The airbrushed surface and cartoonlike rendering of this figurine-size, leafless ceramic tree gives it the characteristics of a mass-produced knickknack that has little in common with nature itself, but instead serves as a token of our reverence for nature's beauty. Its soft, elegant curves and toylike size evoke Disneyesque perfection and simplicity that remove the usual disorder found in nature. The limbs of the tree's two trunks are identical (much like the twin Osage oranges), and are joined at the top, forming an absurd anthropomorphic figure. The miniature tree's twisting limbs and the tabletop container in which it is "planted" recall those of Japanese bonsai—dwarf trees cultivated and trained to grow in desired shapes by the use of wire coils. It is paradoxical that these tiny trees, grown by Buddhists to adorn shrines to the beauty and serenity of nature, are subjected to such extreme manipulation in pursuit of a "natural," miniaturized stand-in for real, life-size nature. Pierzynski hints that perfection in nature is not only a figment of our imagination but might also become the object of an obsessive fetishization.

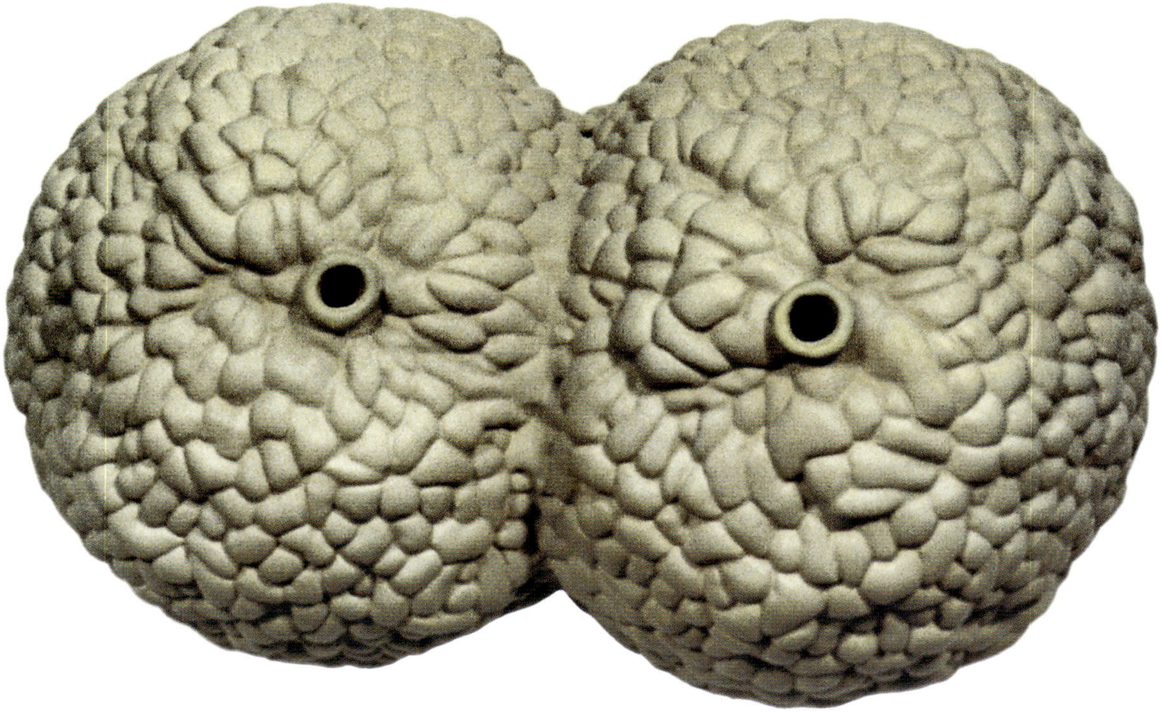

MICHAEL PIERZYNSKI

25. *Untitled*, 2001 (brown)

on facing page:
24. *Cultivating Internal Plastic Infinity*, 1999

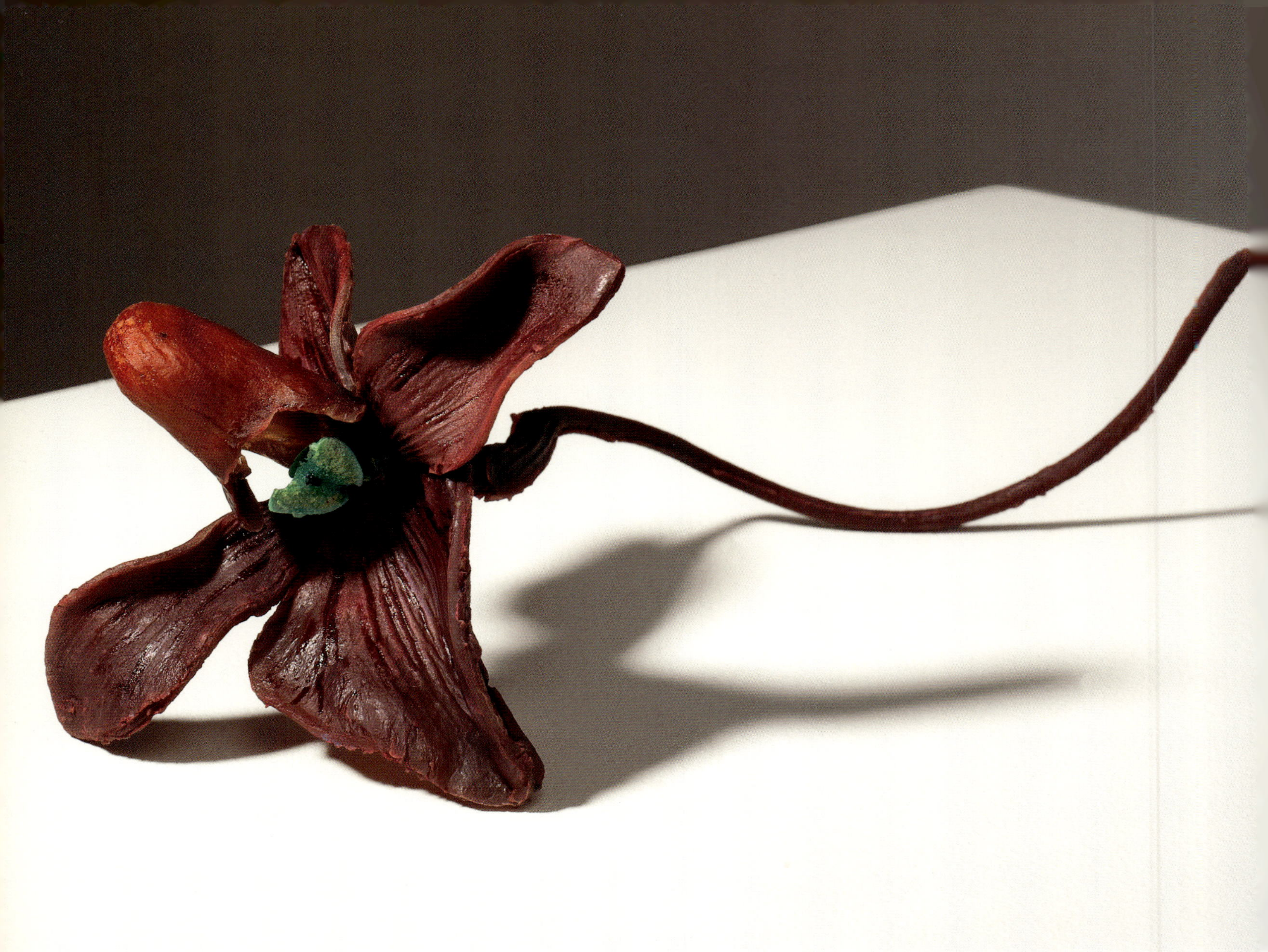

KEITH EDMIER

15. *Keith's Paphiopedilum (Version One)*, 2001

on facing page:
fig. 1. *A Dozen Roses*, 1998
(not in the exhibition)

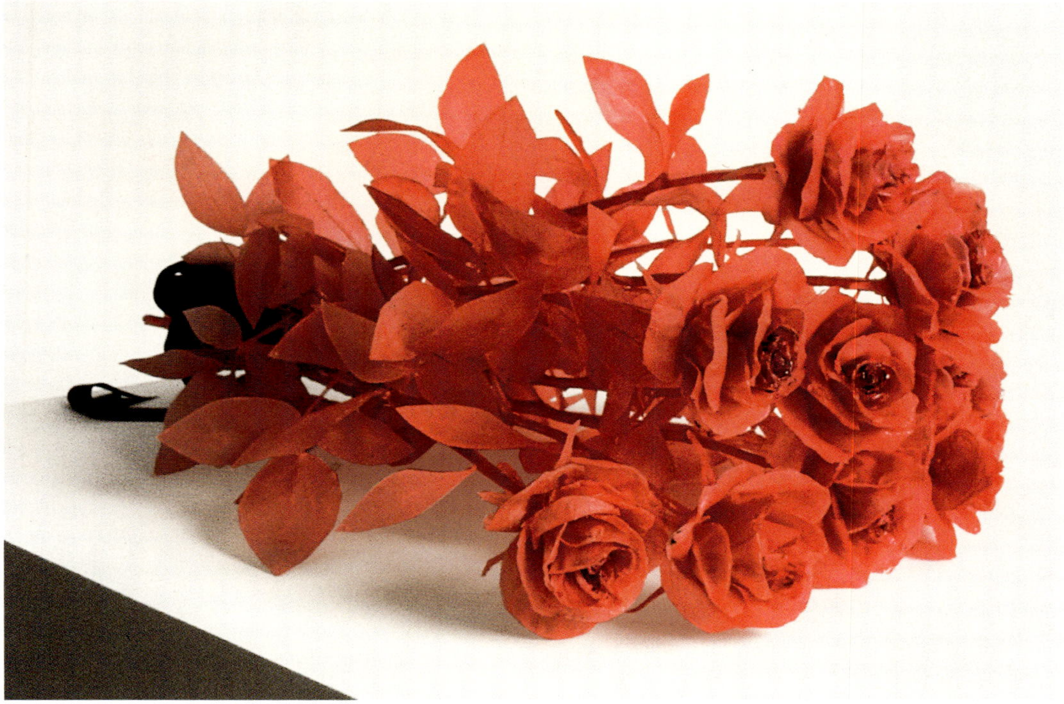



Keith Edmier's work reminds us of the ubiquitous use of images from nature in the merchandizing of sentimentality. Made of cast acrylic, urethane resin, and silicone, his fake-flower sculptures represent products of nature that have long been removed from their original habitat and have taken on their own cultural significance. Orchids and long-stem roses, for instance, which have become generic symbols of romance, are grown in commercial greenhouses and sold at top dollar on occasions such as prom night, Valentine's Day, and Mother's Day. The monochromatic, waxy artificiality of *Keith's Paphiopedilum [Version One]* (cat. no. 15) and *A Dozen Roses* (fig. 1) emphasizes the lack of authenticity in the gesture of giving someone flowers. The real satin ribbon tied to the ends of the plastic roses appears to wilt next to the perky leaves and petals, and reads as a nostalgic reminder of a time before artificial flowers existed and sentiment was not so tainted by notions of Hallmark-card holidays.

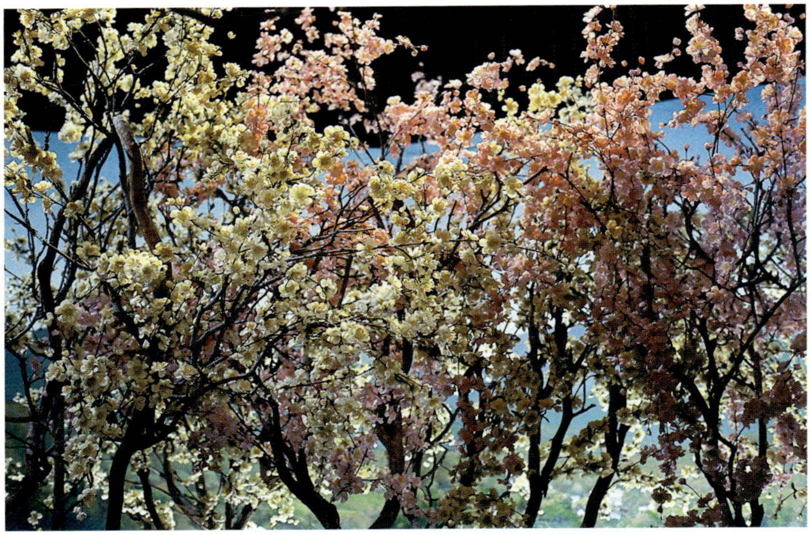

## NATURE ON FILM

By now, people have been conditioned to experience mediated realities through movies, digital imagery, and manipulated photography. As a result, a great deal of artwork being made today shows evidence of an increased attention paid to the issue of fake versus real. Lacking the magic of the latest Hollywood technology, however, artists using photography are faced with the challenge of viewers' waning belief in the validity of the photograph and their close scrutiny of all photographic images. In the game of creating convincing imagery, the motivation for these artists goes beyond entertainment. Often their work is intended to call into question conventional definitions of the real and the simulated.

Los Angeles artist Nicoletta Munroe takes her cues from the entertainment industry by photographing sets from a popular daytime television show in off hours when they're not being used. Working as a free-lance art director, Munroe, like many artists living in close proximity to Hollywood, is privy to the complex machinations of creating visual fiction on film. In her *Cherry Blossoms* series (see cat. nos. 18, 19), she presents treetops in a rural setting that, by degrees, reveals signs of artificiality in the visible seams and loosely painted horizon of the backdrop. The resulting pictures are an intriguing observation of how certain images in still photographs or movies pass for authentic in spite of their obvious fakeness. Her intention is not to trick the average viewer but rather, with a secret wink to those in the know, to expose the Hollywood-industry trade secrets of simulation. Her work takes advantage of lighting, cropping, camera angle, and other factors that all increase the credibility of a set. A hybrid of truth and fiction emerges from the work, asking us to contemplate the ever-diminishing distinction between the two.

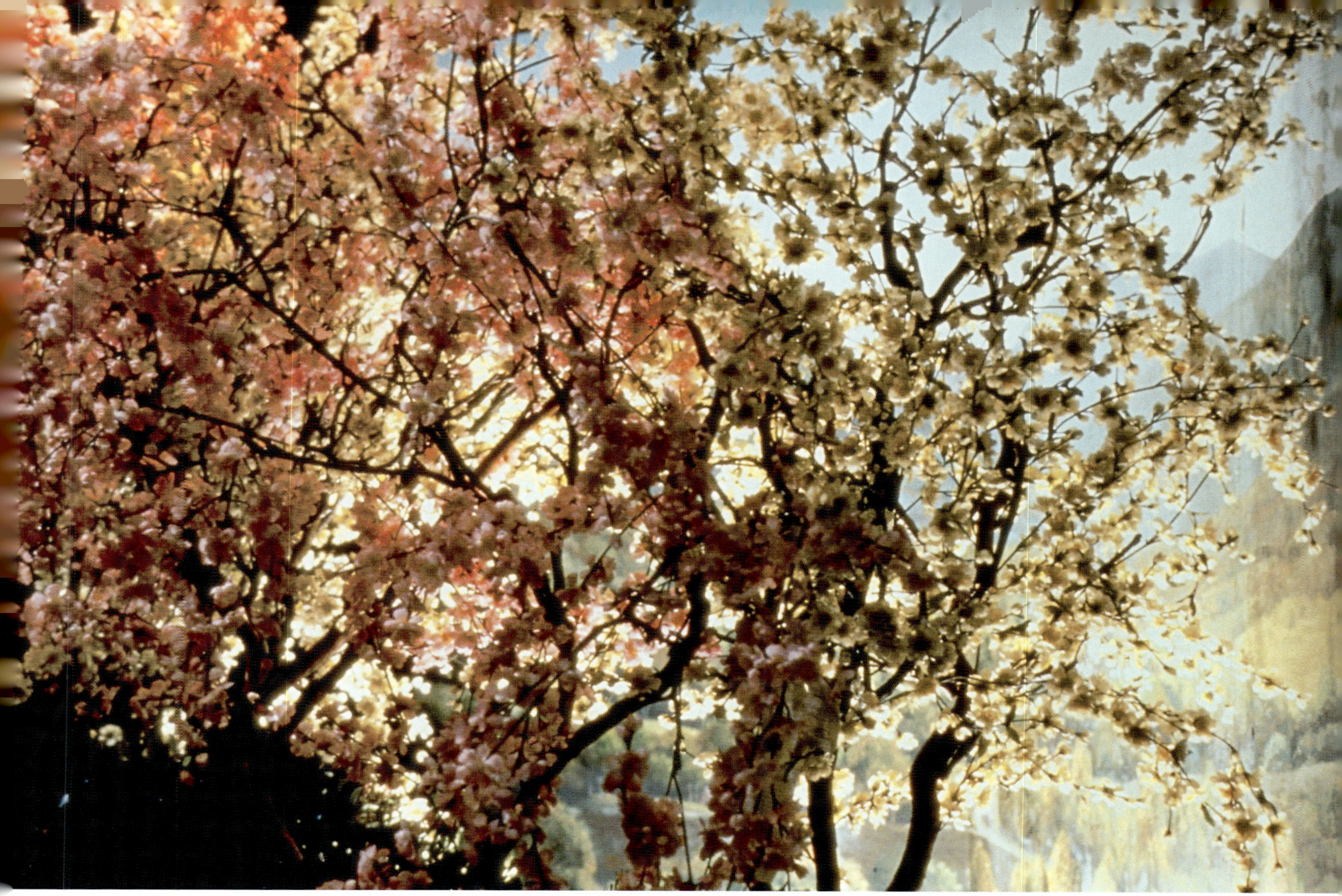

NICOLETTA MUNROE

19. *Cherry Blossoms II (Stage Right)*, 2000

on facing page:
18. *Cherry Blossoms III (Stage Center)*, 2000

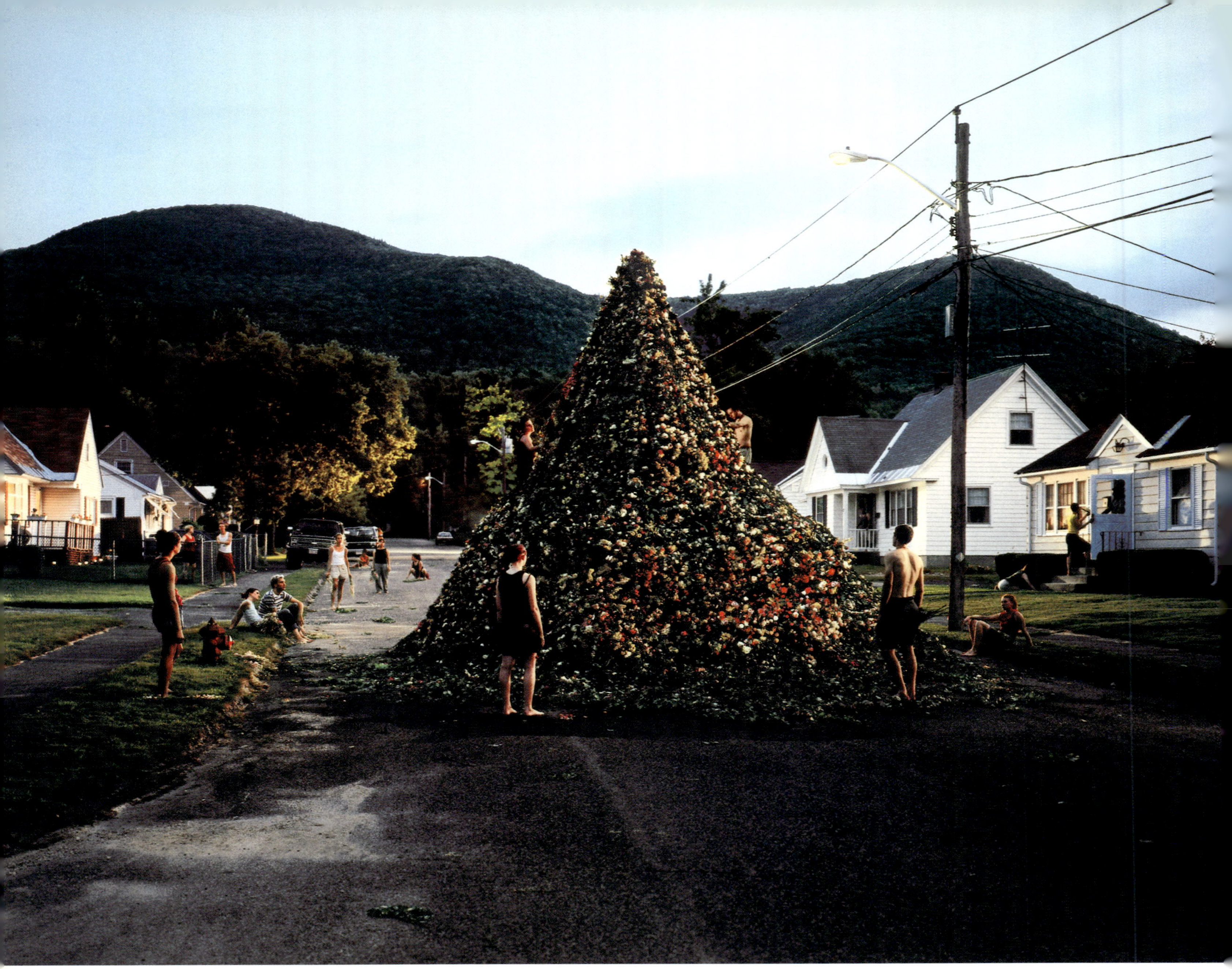

GREGORY CREWDSON

6. *Untitled (Flower Pile)*, 2001

on facing page:
5. *Untitled*
*(Flower Beanstalk)*, 2001

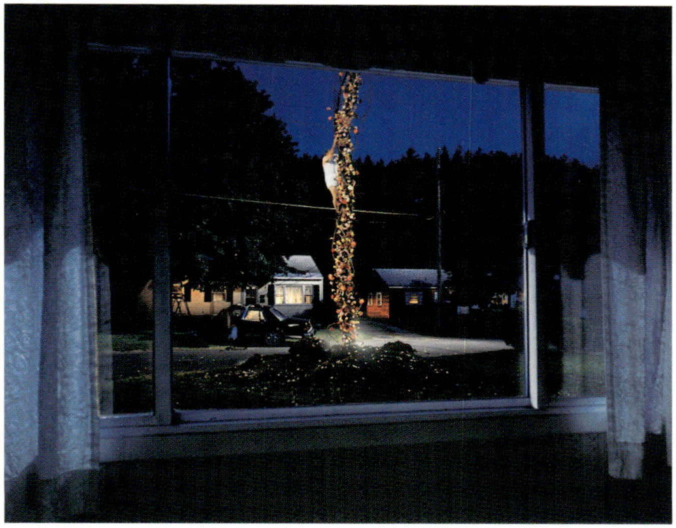

Gregory Crewdson traverses the well-worn territory of simulating nature on film in his most recent series of photographs, entitled *Twilight*. Each of the three photographs from that series included in the exhibition (see cat. nos. 5–7) depicts a moment of a drama occurring in an anonymous suburban setting as if it were suspended in time. Crewdson's elaborately staged scenes express an idea of nature that falls somewhere between reality and imagination. A recent article in the *New York Times Magazine* described Crewdson as being "at the forefront of a movement in contemporary photography that has abandoned realism in the pursuit of pure cinematic fantasy."[2] His strategy of merging the familiar and the surreal are reminiscent of science fiction, and owe as much to the conventions of blockbuster movies as they do to the staged photographs of Jeff Wall and Tina Barney. Like a film director, Crewdson works with a large crew of technical advisors and set designers in order to take full advantage of the film industry's ability to turn imaginary situations into realistic-looking scenes. The strange, fantastic world he fabricates—at once obviously artificial and surprisingly naturalistic—captivates the viewer in the same way that a frightening fairy tale enthralls a child, with amazing images of nature's mysterious powers that feed into, and are compounded by, our imaginations.

2. *Deborah Solomon, "The Ultimate Film Still,"* NEW YORK TIMES MAGAZINE, *March 25, 2001, p. 51.*

Two other artists in the exhibition, Chris Astley and Allan deSouza, make photographs of their own constructed scenes that, unlike Crewdson's life-size tableaux of recognizable places, are miniature sets depicting imaginary natural settings. Once again, the power of the photographed image to convince

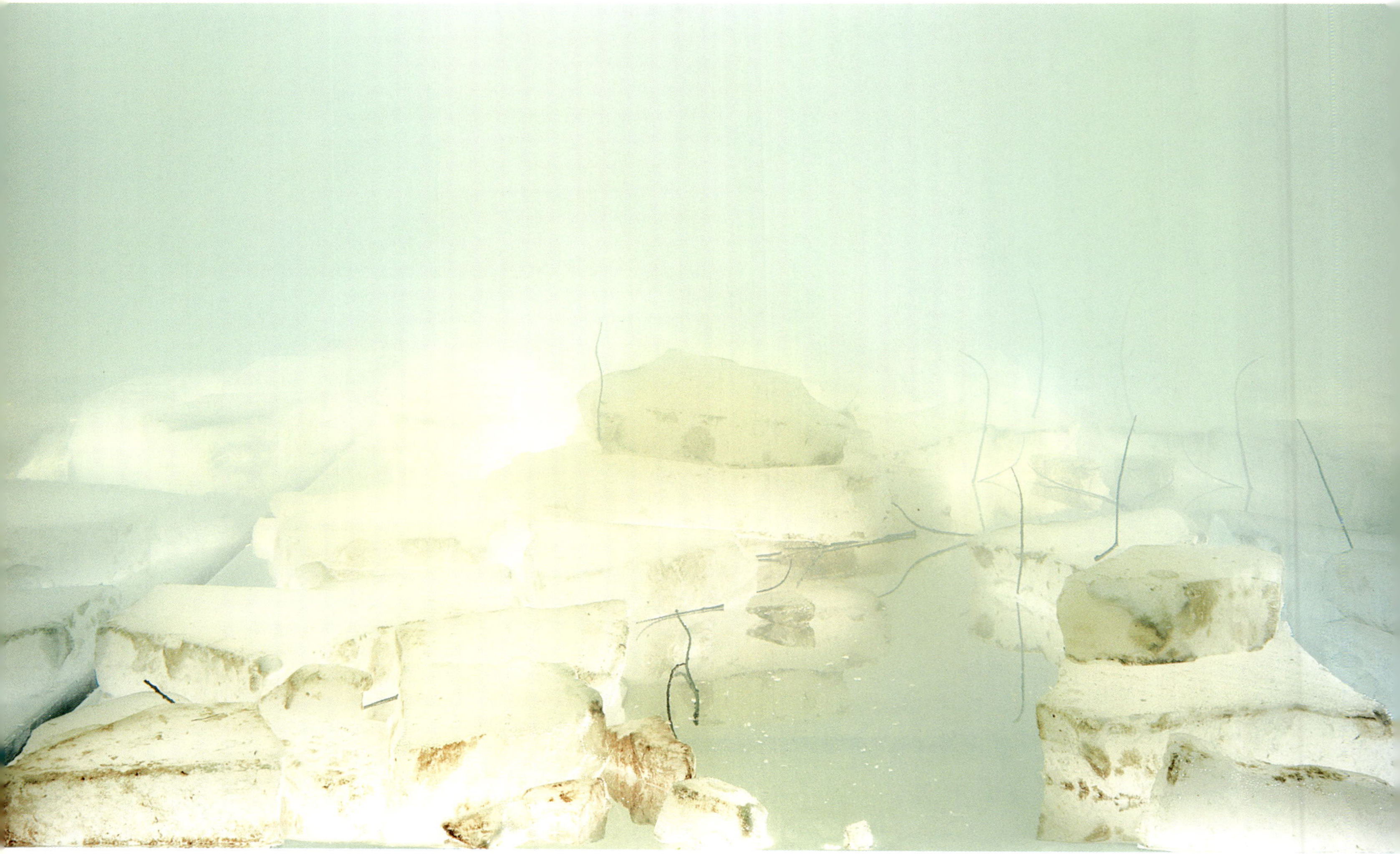

1.
CHRIS ASTLEY
*Volume IV*, 2000

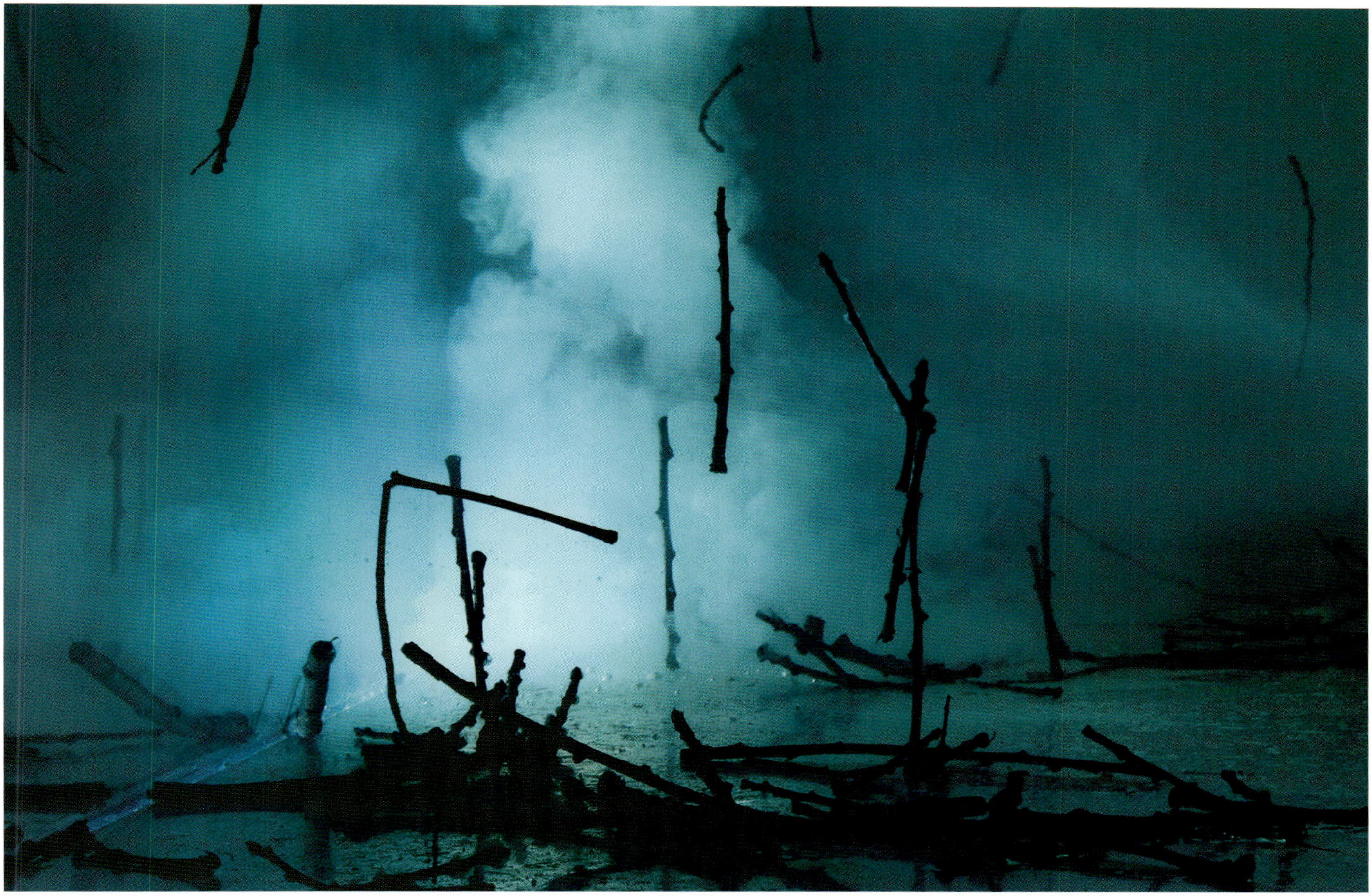

3.
CHRIS ASTLEY
*Volume VI*, 2000

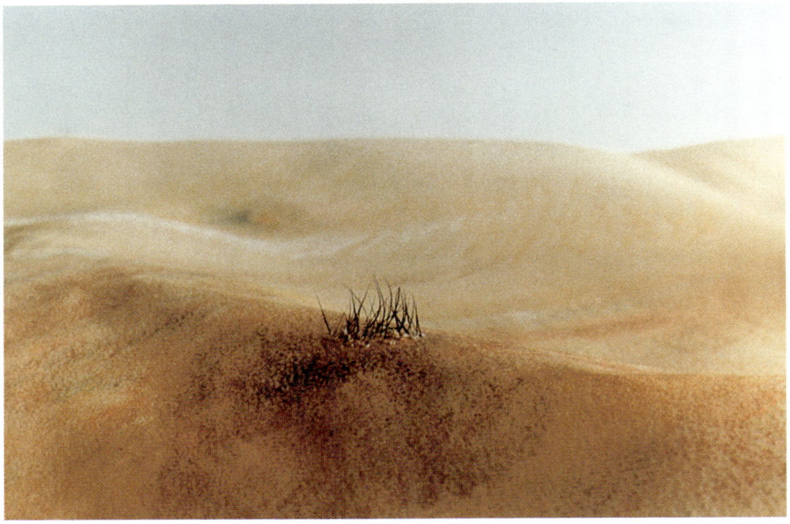

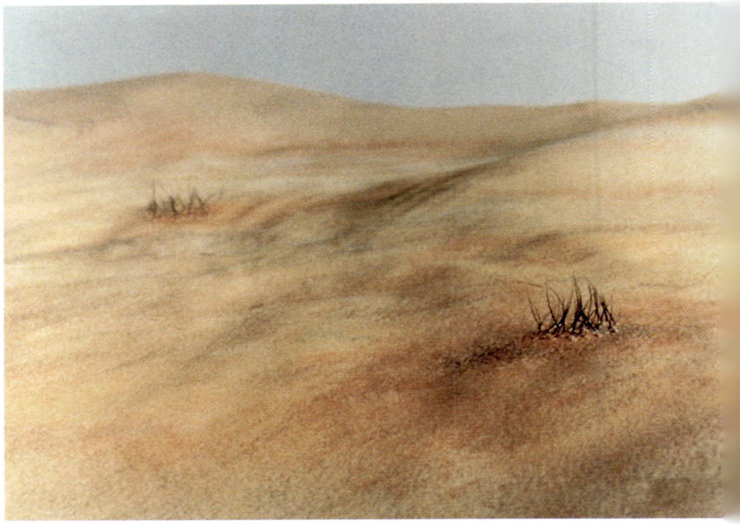

us of authenticity is put to the test as the artists attempt to bring their subjects to life through the lens of the camera. Astley's photographs are filled with suspended branches, mysterious vapors and fluids, and translucent blocks, as in *Volume IV* (cat. no. 1). The compressed, foreshortened space and murky atmosphere in the images evoke a tranquil, eerie mood that invites us to ruminate. One wonders if the artist has come across this scene in the landscape, or if he manipulated nature in a controlled environment to produce these dreamy images. Are we looking at a harmless science project in an aquarium, or through a window onto untamed wilderness? Astley deliberately camouflages any clues that might help determine the scale or identify the scene. His provocative results challenge viewers to carefully inspect each photograph for signs of intervention or manipulation, and thus question their own perception of reality.

DeSouza's beguiling series *Terrain* (cat. nos. 12–14) features "landscapes" that he has shot using makeshift models assembled from a random collection of ordinary materials such as painted paper and from remnants of his own body, including nail clippings, ear wax, and eyelashes. Like Astley, his interest lies in the ambiguity of scale and reinvention of space produced by low-tech methods of sheer fakery. Once photographed, deSouza's deliberately rudimentary dioramas look like faraway or mythical lands devoid of any sign of human life. Yet the earth tones of the barren hills evoke the surface of skin, and the tumbleweeds appear suspiciously similar to patches of human hair. These inde-

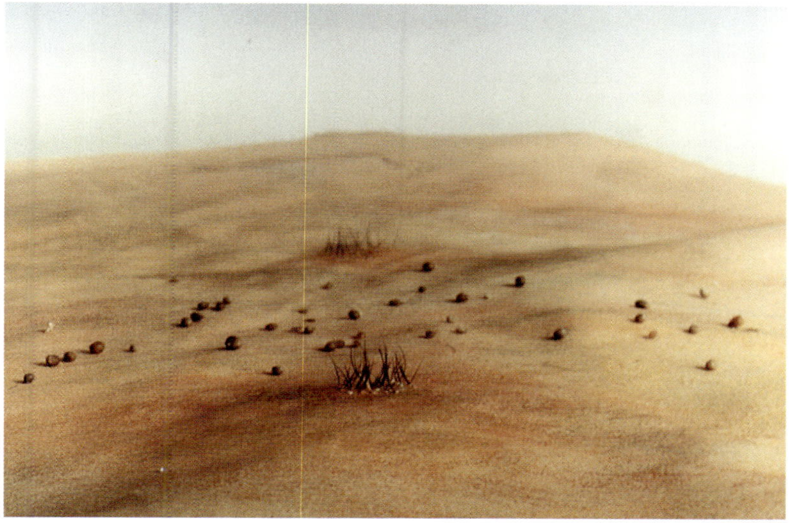

12.–14.
ALLAN DESOUZA
*Terrain #5, #7, #8,*
1999–2000



terminate images create a familiar dichotomy of microcosm (ourselves) and macrocosm (our surroundings), reminding us of our symbiotic relationship with nature. The *Terrain* series also makes reference to the notion of nature as a sublime force that is at once vast and omnipotent yet intimate and fragile.

Marc Quinn strives to improve on the beauty of nature by "preserving" life and thus escaping the usually unavoidable onset of decay. For *Garden$^2$*, a suite of eight pigment prints (cat. no. 28), he photographed an installation he created in 2001 entitled *Garden*, in which he filled an enormous aquarium with exotic plants that were collected from all parts of the globe and then submerged them in silicon. Quinn, who is known for his investigations into scientific manipulation and the human desire to prevail over nature, seems determined to achieve unattainable perfection. Talking about *Garden* in a recent interview, he explained the paradox of this elusive paradise: "The flowers are perfect and will last forever, but obviously they are dead: they've been turned into icons, just like movie or pop stars who die young. We continue to worship their perfect image, but, for them, it's all over."[3] The supersaturated, Day-Glo colors and shining, waxy surfaces of the plants give the impression that we are looking at something completely artificial. Even though they are real, there is an inherent artificiality in the eternally "frozen" preservation of the plants and the unnatural juxtaposition of different species from far-flung regions of the earth. Quinn guilefully illustrates the conundrum that gardens exist to meet human demand and require nature to succumb to human will.

*3. Quinn, quoted in Germano Celant, "Interview with Marc Quinn," in* MARC QUINN, *exh. cat. (Milan: Prada Foundation, 2000), p. 214.*

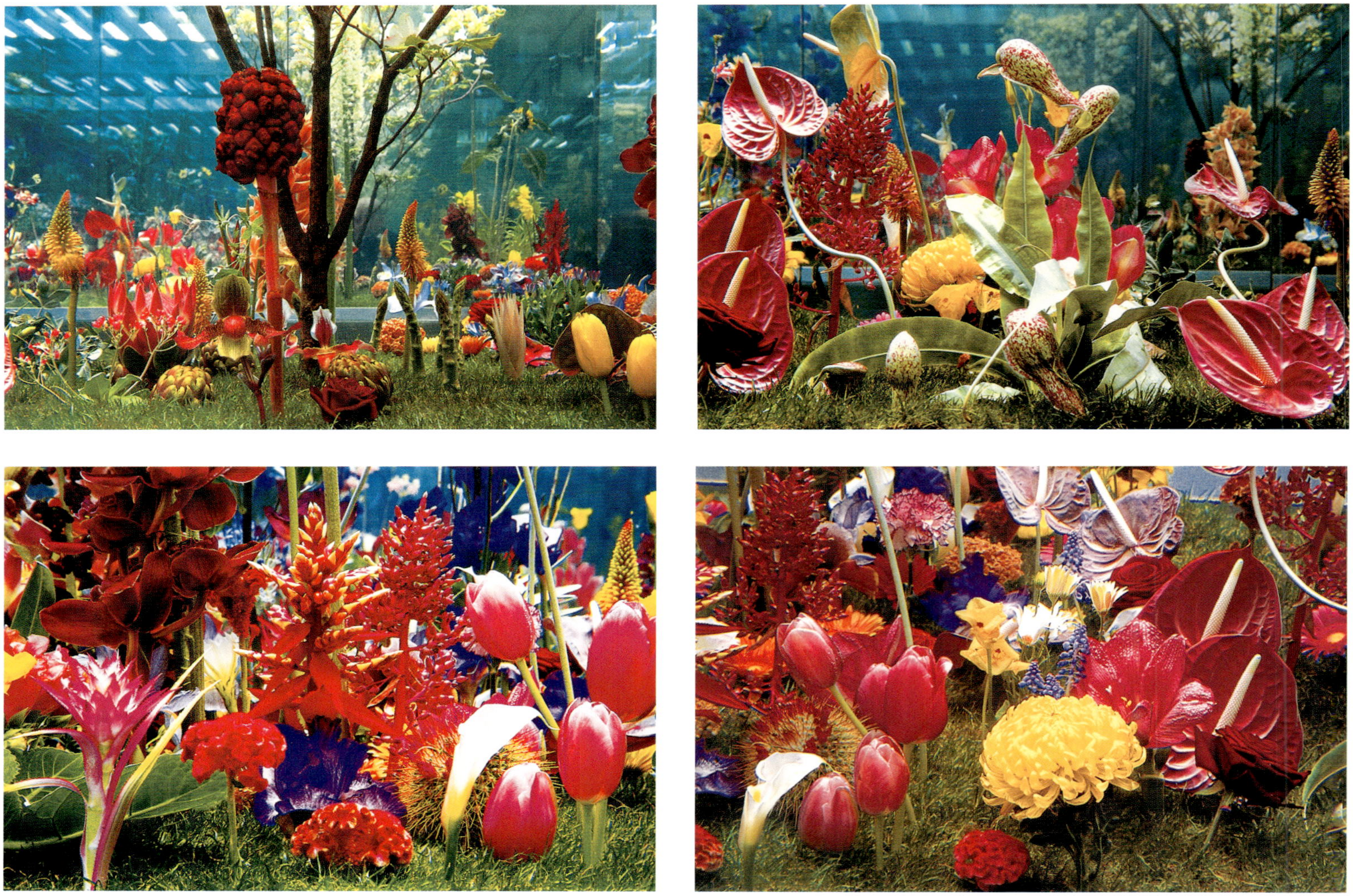

28.
MARC QUINN
*Garden*$^2$, 2000

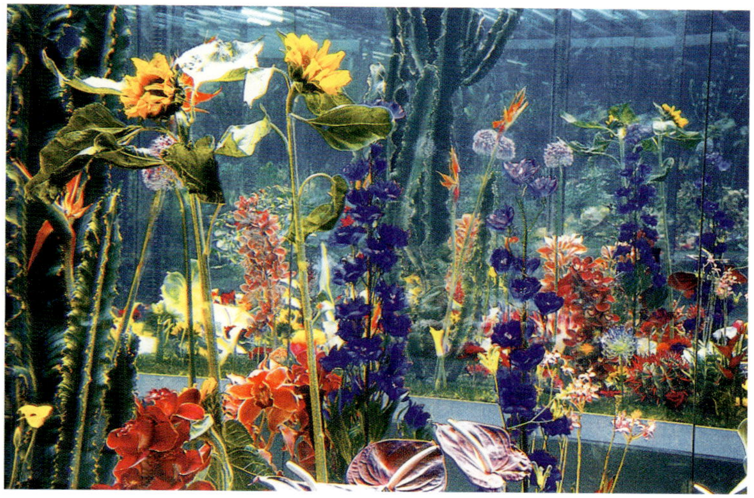
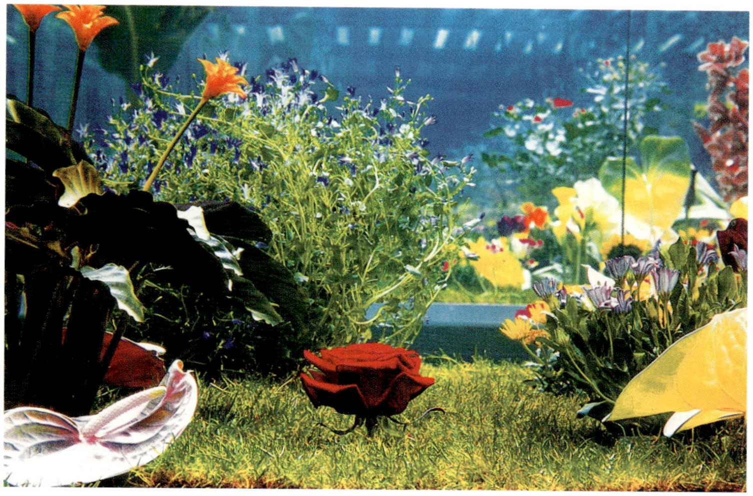
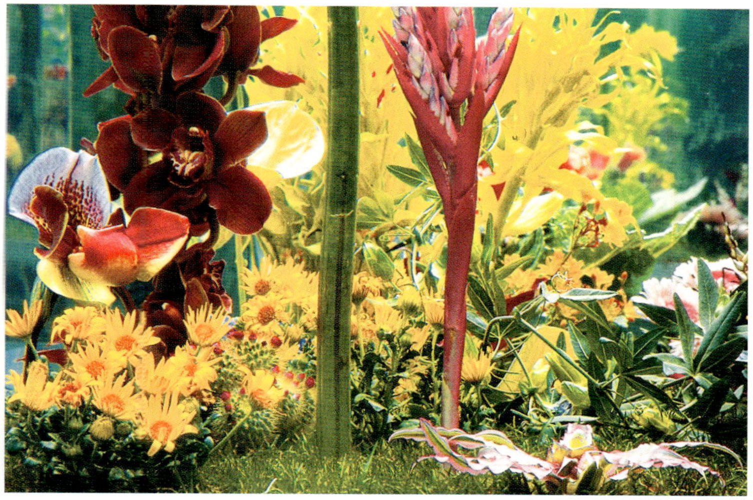
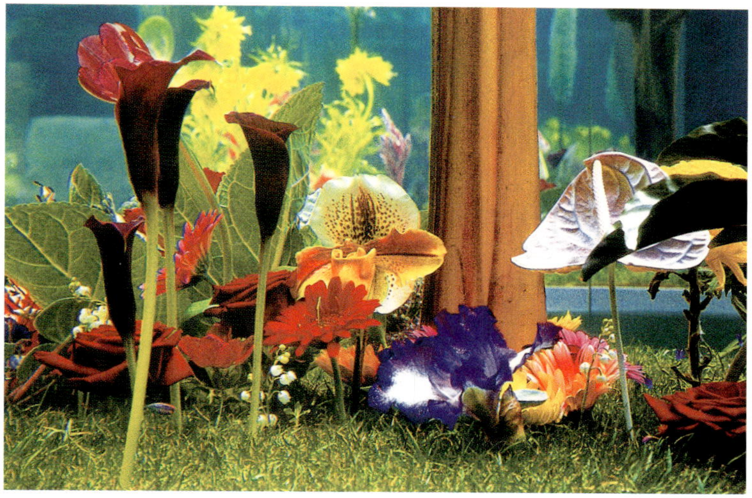

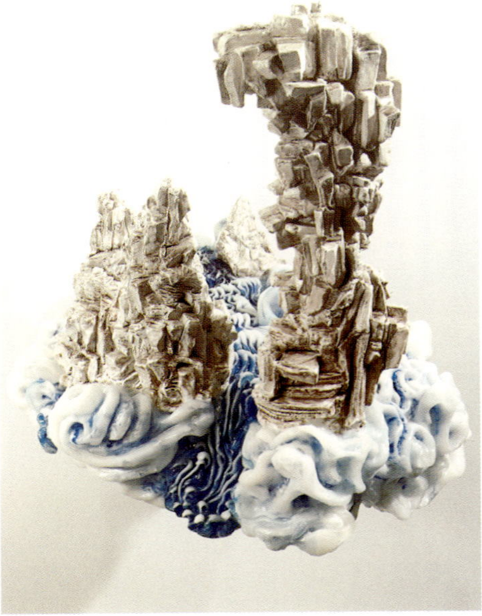



## NATURE IN 3-D

According to *Los Angeles Times* art critic David Pagel, Jacci Den Hartog belongs to a group of artists working in Los Angeles in the evolving genre of landscape sculpture.[4] Den Hartog's seductive work pays homage to ancient Chinese landscape paintings and other two-dimensional representations of nature. The luscious objects she makes, depicting rock-faced mountains and flowing, frothy water, evoke the power and beauty of nature rather than re-creating it with exactitude. The slick, synthetic surfaces of these works reveal both a mastery of artifice and a dual interest in popular culture and art-historical traditions. Made of polyurethane-coated plaster, these frozen replicas are fantastical interpretations of nature that revel in their deliberate artificiality, such as *Passing a Pleasant Summer II* or *Garden for Walking Through Water* (cat. nos. 7, 9). As Pagel wrote, "Being fake takes nothing away from [these] sensuous sculptures. In fact, by shamelessly embracing fakery, Den Hartog intensifies the effects her miniature mountains have on the viewers."[5] The unnaturalness of the sculptures is emphasized by the presentation of these chunks of land and sea in a gallery setting. Perched on a steel-pole pedestal or mounted on a white wall, each curling wave and jagged rock formation becomes an emblem of the dislocation between unfettered nature and urban life.

Frances Whitehead's work demonstrates an abiding concern with the ways in which new technology and industry affect our relationship with the natural world. Growing and maintaining a garden in the back yard of her house in Chicago has led her to an in-depth investigation of the scientific system of classifying and naming plants according to their presumed natural relationships. In a new series of drawings and related sculptures, Whitehead has rendered poppies as geometric forms modeled in the virtual space of 3-D software. The resultant images, which combine graph lines and measurements with intricate patterns and buoyant, domelike shapes, look more like technical drawings for manufactured objects and only vaguely resemble the original flowers

4. *David Pagel, "Entering a New Dimension,"* LOS ANGELES TIMES, *August 25, 1996, p. 7.*

5. *Ibid.*

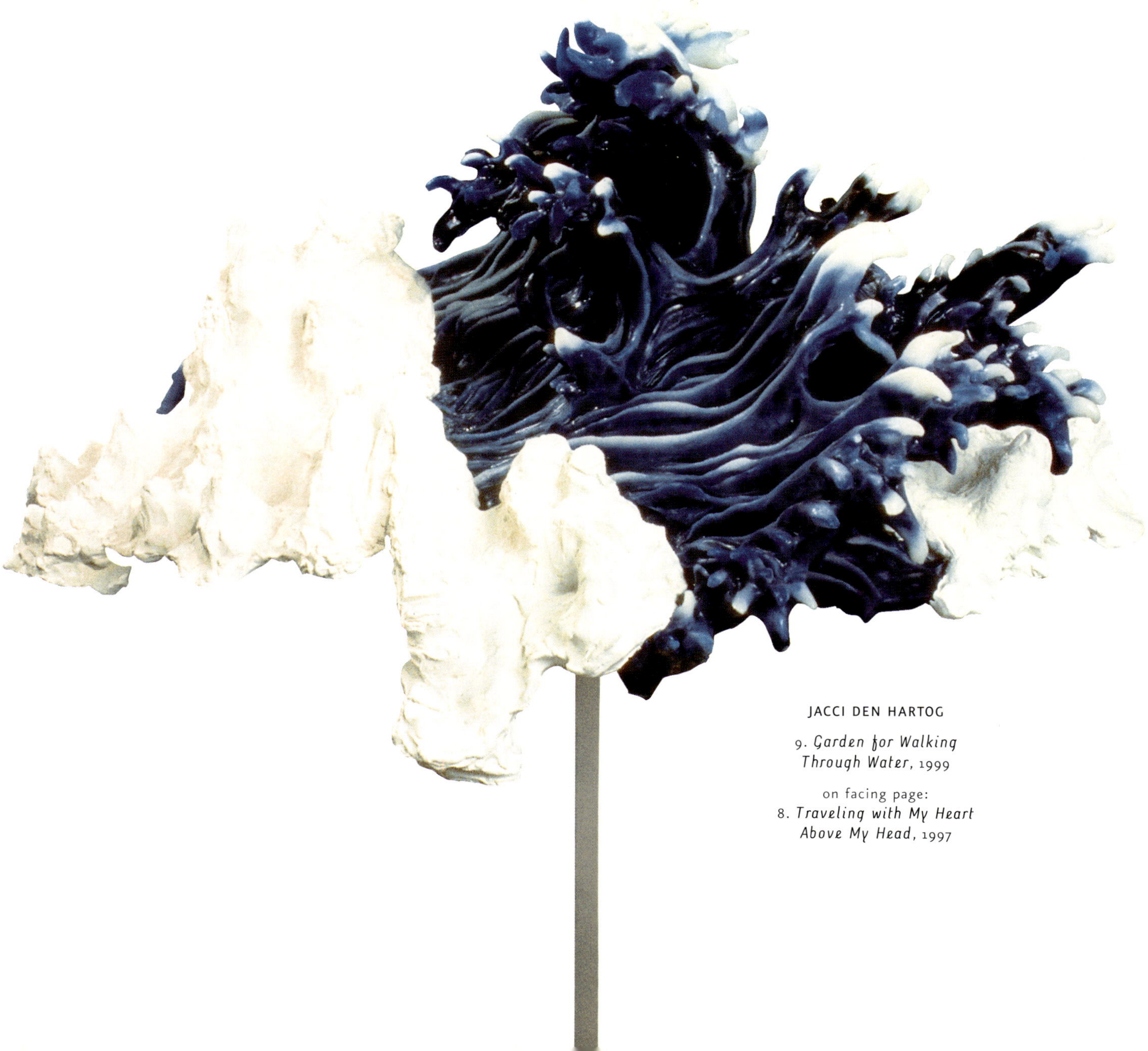

JACCI DEN HARTOG

9. *Garden for Walking Through Water*, 1999

on facing page:
8. *Traveling with My Heart Above My Head*, 1997

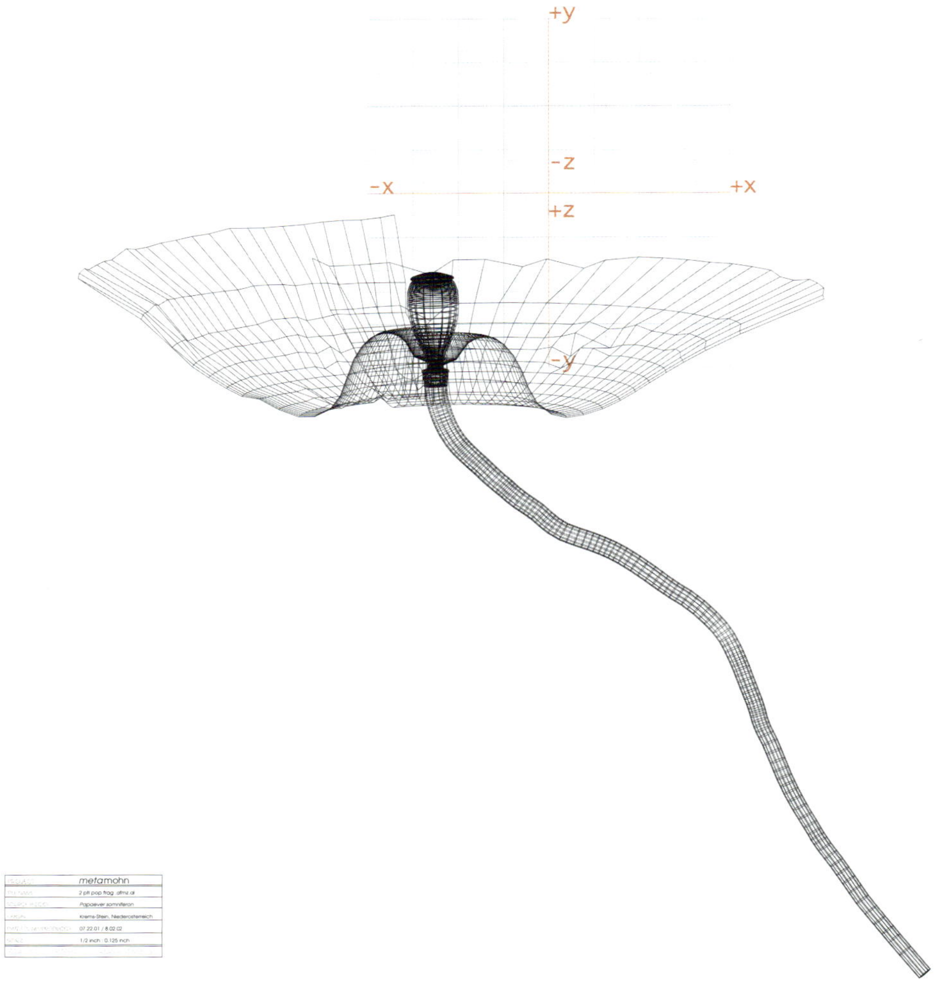


FRANCES WHITEHEAD

40. *metamohn.2ptl pop frag.afmz.ai*, 2001

below:
41. *metamohn.2ptl pop frag.afmz.stl*, 2001

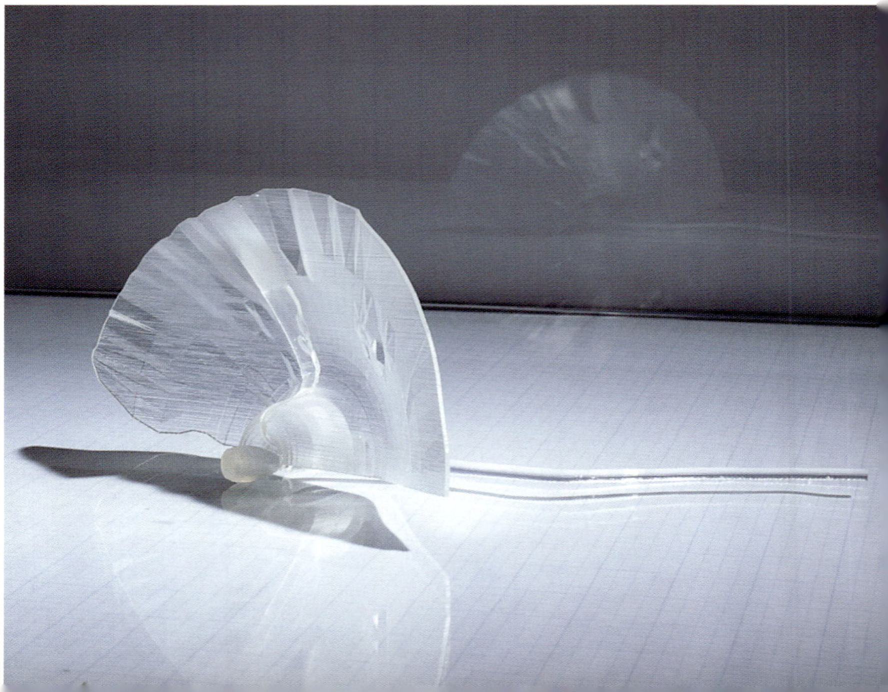

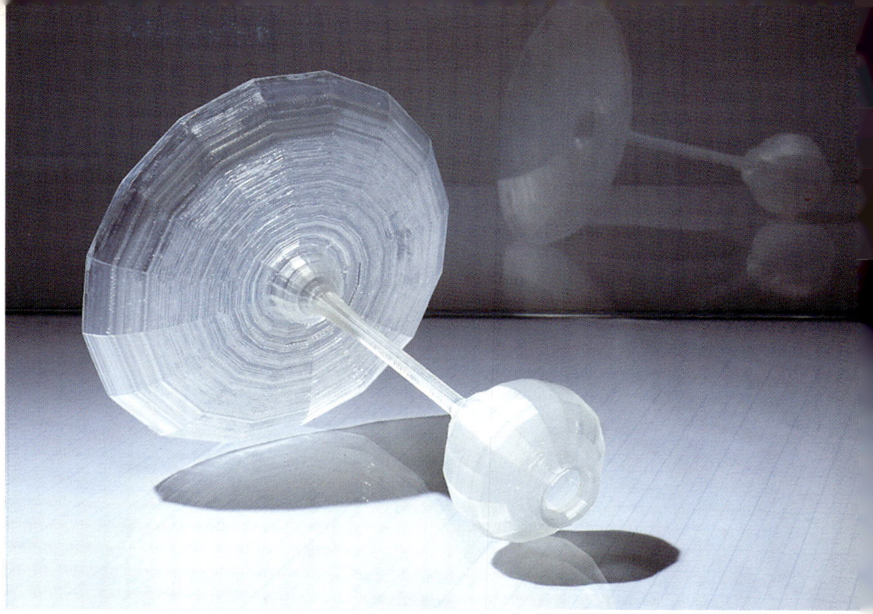

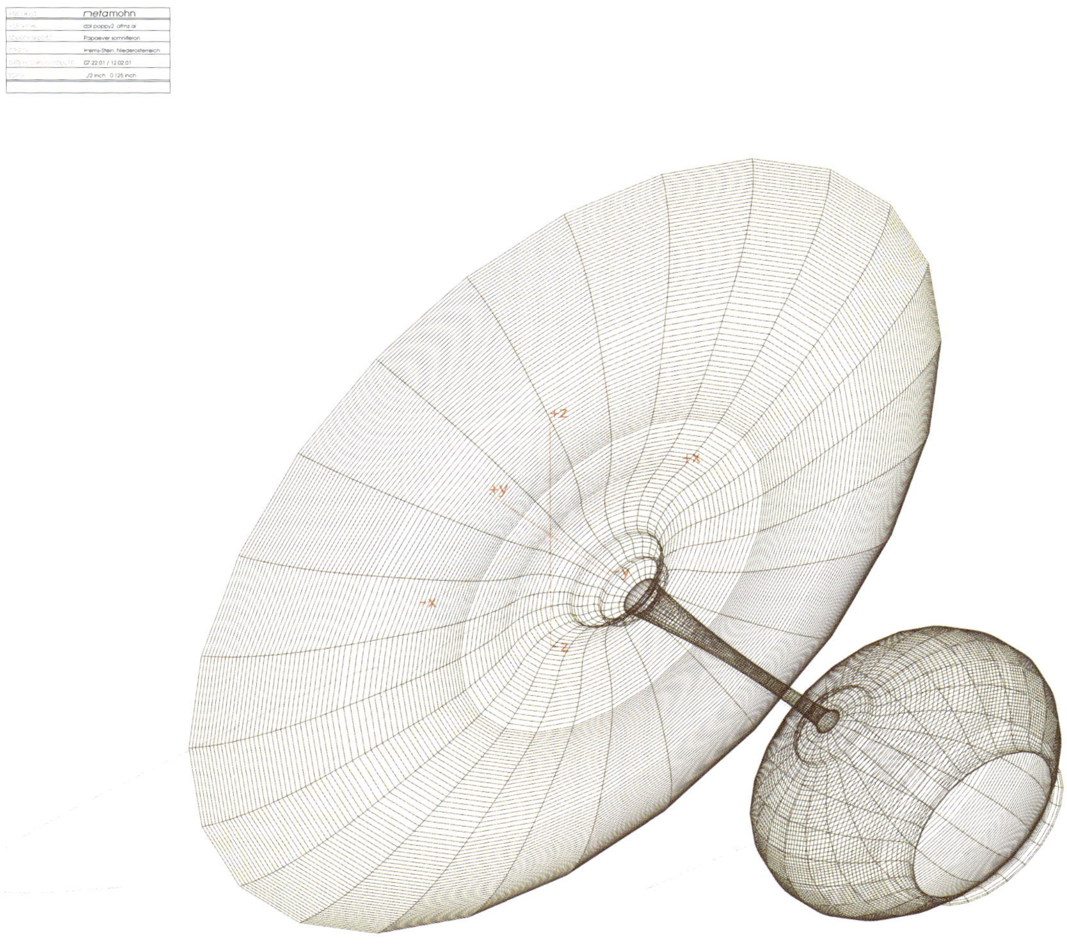


FRANCES WHITEHEAD

above:
37. *metamohn.dbl pop2.afmz.stl*, 2001

36. *metamohn.dbl pop2.afmz.ai*, 2001

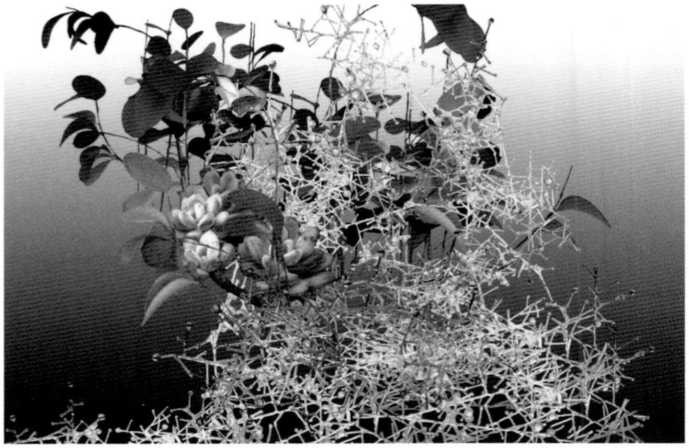



that inspired them. The files that create the drawings are then entered into a rapid-prototyping machine that reads the data and translates the computer-generated forms into three-dimensional objects made of epoxy resin. Whitehead's direct involvement in the modeling of her creative output has thus been removed, replaced by the computer and its peripheral equipment, which fabricated the data output as sculptural replicas. Although they are products of a collaboration between artist and machine, they look wholly mass-produced. These "post-natural" flower forms are strangely seductive and beckon us toward a sci-fi future in which the dichotomy between nature and artifice is completely transcended.

In her titles for these works, Whitehead alludes to the pervasiveness of computers in everyday life by imitating cryptically abbreviated computer-file names with a somewhat scientific aura, such as *metamohn.dbl pop2.afmz.ai* and *metamohn.2ptl pop frag.afmz.stl* (cat. nos. 36, 41). Moreover, she presents the drawings and sculptures in an installation that mimics both the scientific approach and the slickness of contemporary natural-history exhibits: the drawings are digitally printed on backlit film and displayed next to a Plexiglas vitrine containing the sculptures, which are laid out on their sides like botanical specimens. These offer a subtle critique of the assumptions underlying taxonomic classification as well as of art-historical texts and museological methods of display.

## NATURE IN WONDERLAND

Alyson Shotz creates hybrid forms that oscillate between the virtual and the artificial and seem to float in an ambiguous, fictional space. In a series of digitally manipulated Lambda prints entitled *False Branches* (cat. nos. 31, 32), Shotz, who is fascinated with genetic alteration, merges computer-generated imagery with photographs of real forms from nature. Shotz also addresses this issue in her multi-media installation *Still Life* (cat.

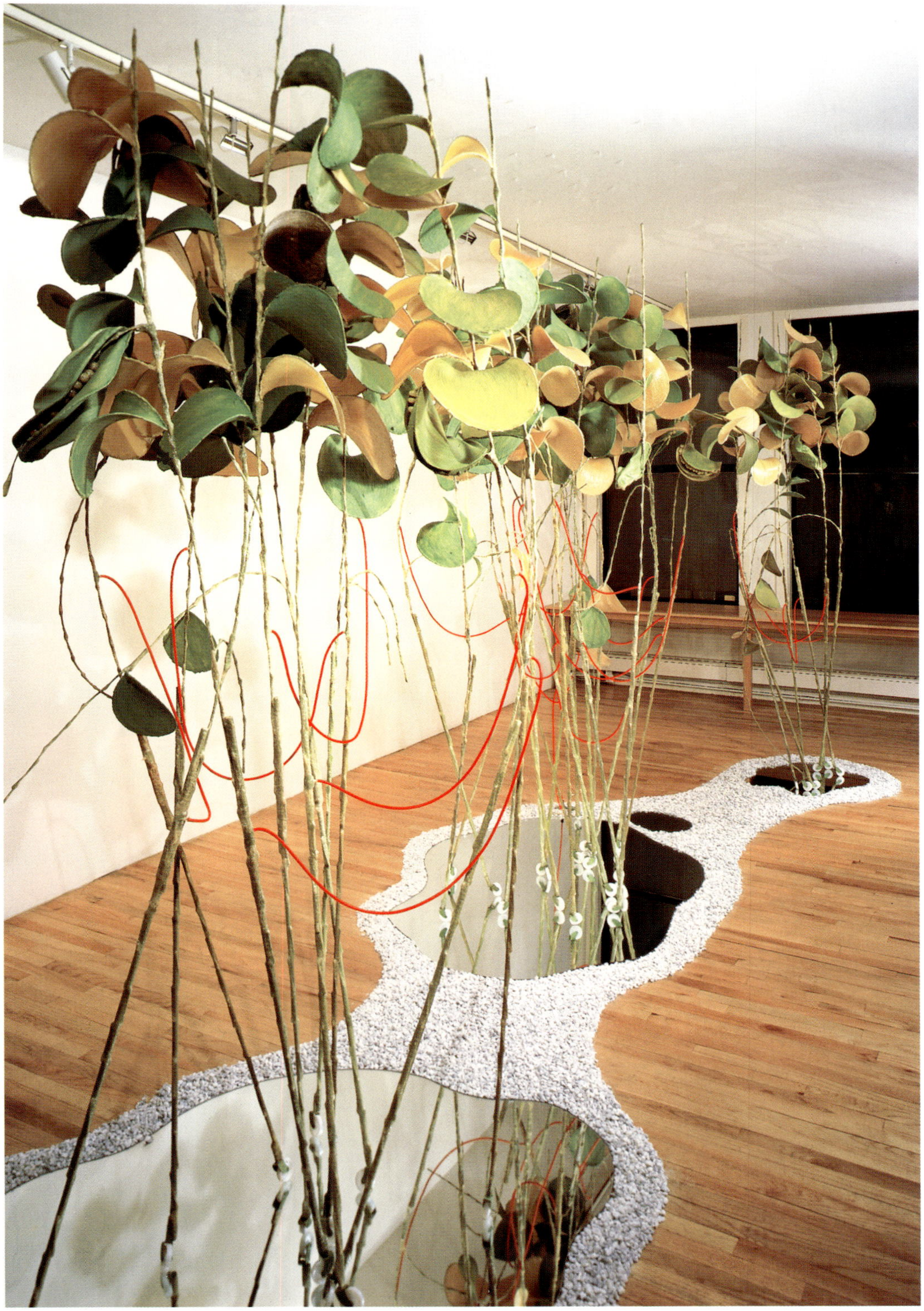

ALYSON SHOTZ

33. *Still Life*, 2001

on facing page:
32. *False Branches #5*, 2001

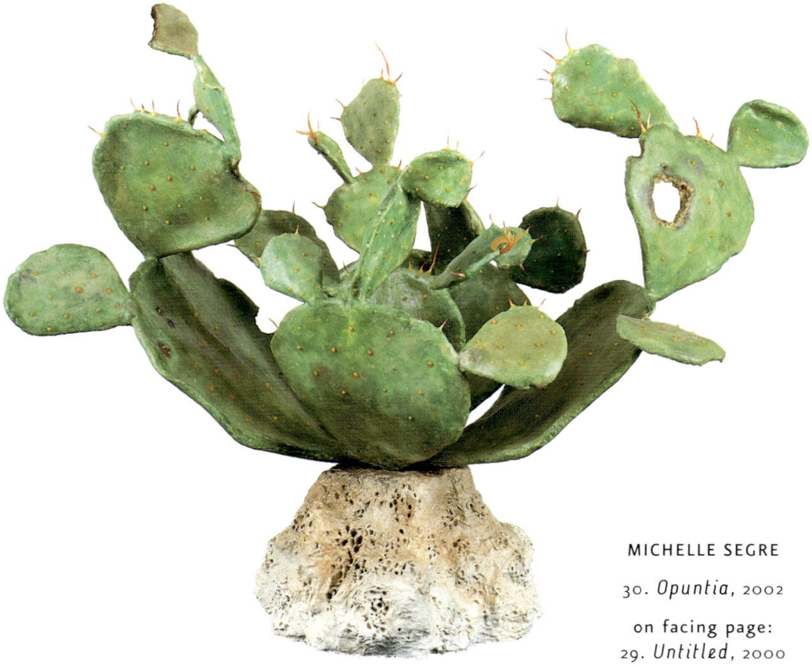

MICHELLE SEGRE

30. *Opuntia*, 2002

on facing page:
29. *Untitled*, 2000

no. 33), which she created using low-tech means and ordinary materials such as wire, gravel, and cotton swabs. Here, oversize leaves and cartoonish pods sprout from gangly, nine-foot-high stalks that bring to mind the strange landscape of a make-believe land. Schotz's invented grove is situated on three free-form, puddlelike mirrors that serve as literal reflecting pools. Rubber tubing dangles from the stalks, which teeter on small, plastic wheels. This mixture of machine-made materials and whimsical, biomorphic shapes pokes fun at the menacing threat of bio-engineering, and suggests the artist playing the role of a mad scientist with a penchant for childlike fantasy.

Michelle Segre's oversize sculptures of plant specimens celebrate the exotic beauty and elegance found in nature's forms. Segre magnifies their sensuous attributes and emphasizes their playful shapes, transforming the everyday into the mythical. By enlarging an ordinary fungus to the size of a person and zooming in on a macroscopic view of its underside, as in *Untitled* (cat. no. 29), she leads the viewer to fortuitous discoveries of details that have been there all along. In *Opuntia* (cat. no. 30), a prickly pear cactus appears exotic not only for its strange shape but also for its seeming ability to grow magically out of a porous rock. Made from beeswax and papier-mâché, Segre's work retains the organic characteristics of her subjects in the fragrance of the wax and the sculptures' tactile surface. Like Alice walking through the looking glass, the viewer enters into a world of full of vivid images where curiosity and a deep appreciation of our surroundings yield spectacular rewards.

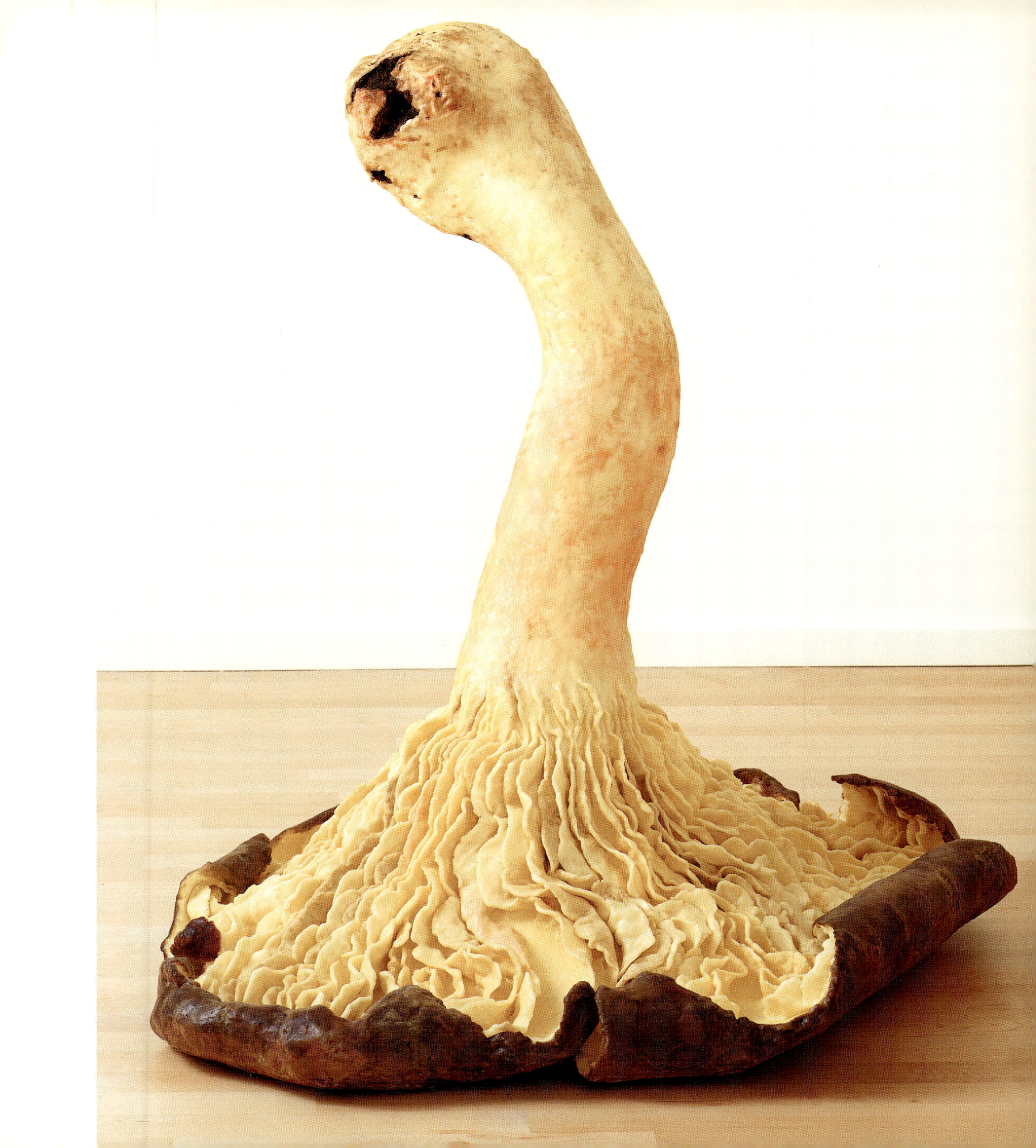

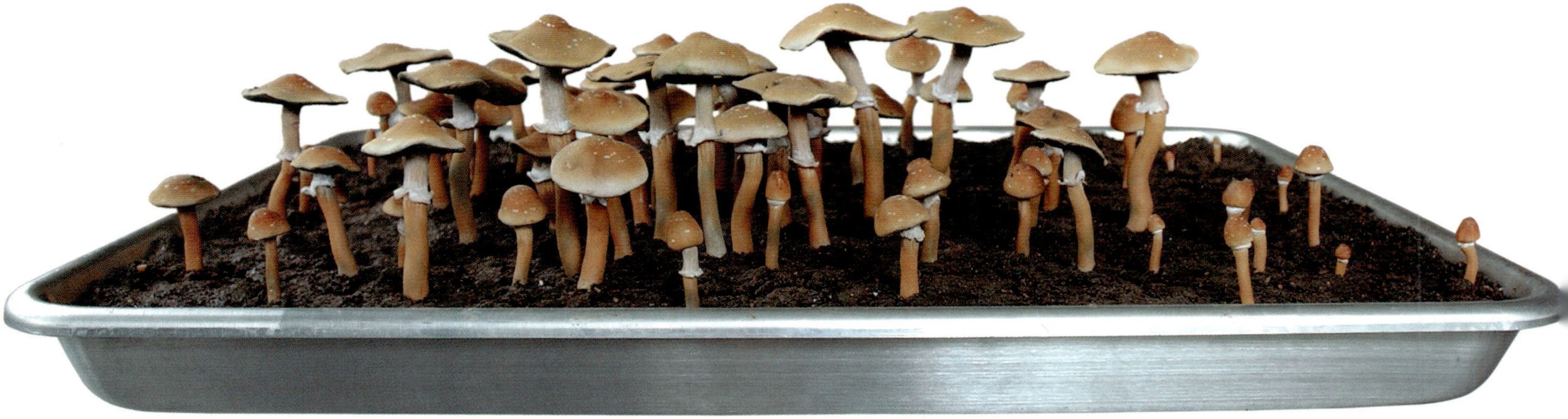

ROXY PAINE

21. *Psilocybe Cubensis Tray*, 1997

on facing page:
20. *Tapioca Slime Painting*, 2001

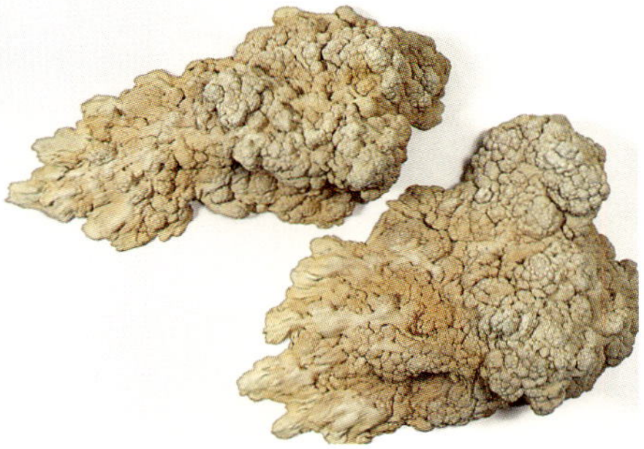

## NATURE BY PROXY



Roxy Paine's imitations of mushrooms, fungi, and other plants appear incredibly real, ironically suggesting that elements of nature can be replaced by man-made replicas. The uncanny accuracy with which the work is rendered belies realism in favor of creating a surrogate for nature as it disappears from everyday, urban experience. Using steel, epoxy, Thermoset plastic, and other "unnatural" materials, Paine painstakingly hand-models and hand-paints each specimen in order to re-create every detail of various botanicals. He sets up a tension between the vast world of nature and our struggle to understand, and perhaps control it, by reproducing it exactly. While the work is visually compelling and pleasurable to look at, it is also strangely unsettling. In *Psilocybe Cubensis Tray* (cat. no. 21), Paine presents a species of mushroom that has hallucinogenic properties, pointedly alluding to the possibility of an altered state of consciousness, and more generally implying a subtext of decay and degeneration. However, these organic cycles of nature are divorced from their natural environment. The mushrooms, contained in a large metal tray and enshrined in Plexiglas for our viewing pleasure, are once removed from the danger of nature in the wild.

Up-ending the staid order of the art-museum environment, Paine reproduces these irregular forms en masse and displays them as if they are growing right out of the gallery wall. In *Tapioca Slime Painting* (cat. no. 20), he directly addresses the art world by presenting a plain stretched canvas being overrun by a thick glob of organic matter spreading across the otherwise clean, white surface. In this clever send-up of abstract painting, Paine comments on the absurdity of the artist's hand occupying a place of privilege in our culture and suggests that natural growth can often create a more compelling surface and composition.

Jason Middlebrook shares with Paine an interest in both the definition of abstraction and the concept of nature encroaching on culture's stronghold and reclaiming our man-made environment. Middlebrook, the son of a stone

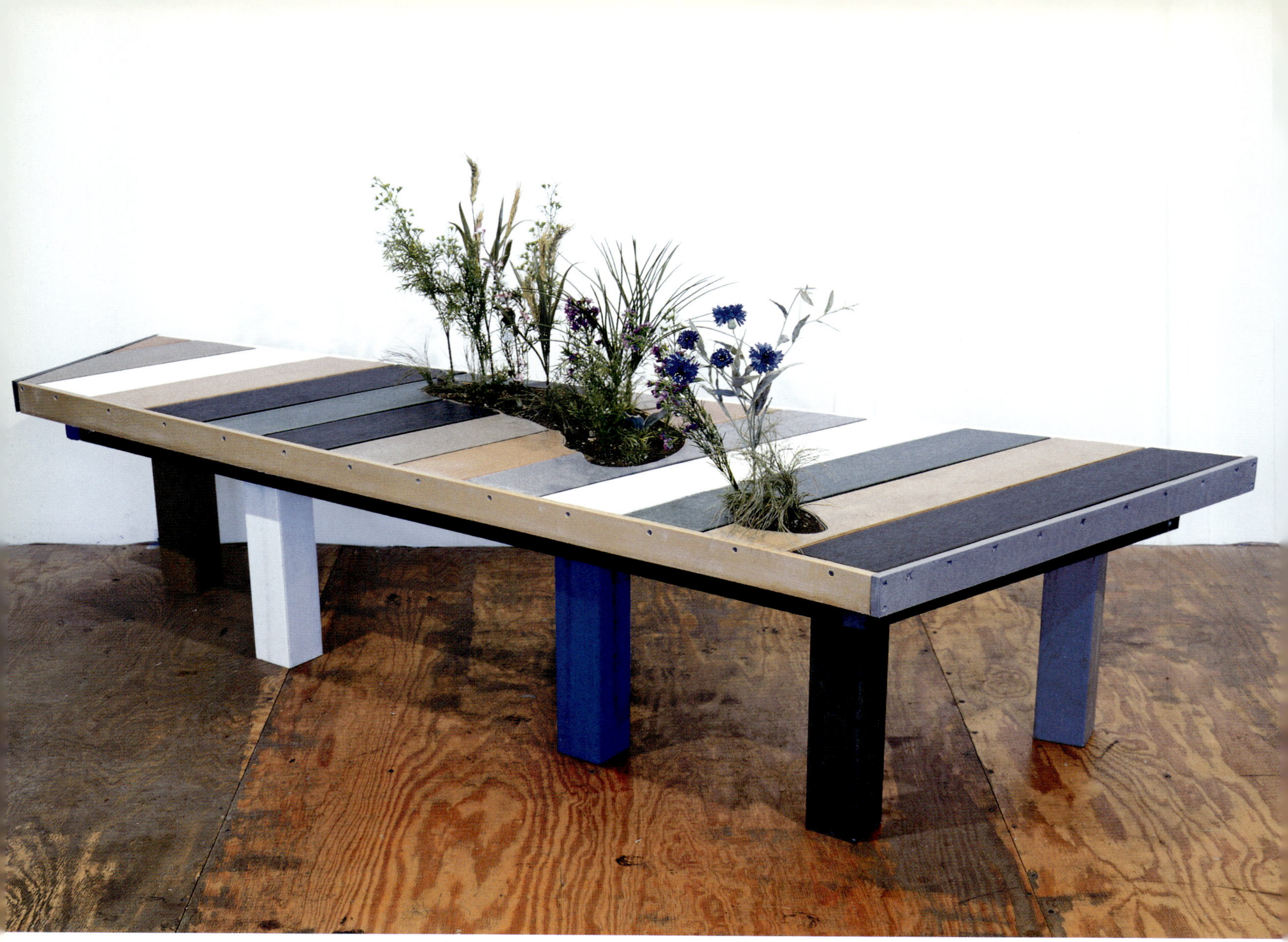

17.
JASON MIDDLEBROOK
*Plant*, 2002 (detail)

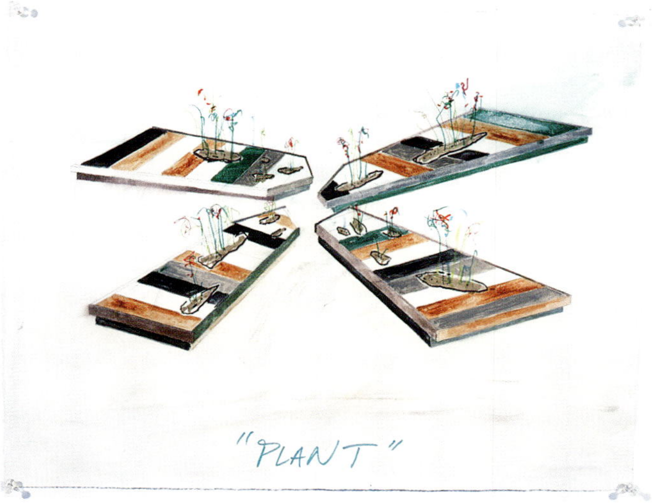


JASON MIDDLEBROOK

fig. 2. Study for *Plant*, 2002
(not in the exhibition)

below:
17. *Plant*, 2002 (detail)

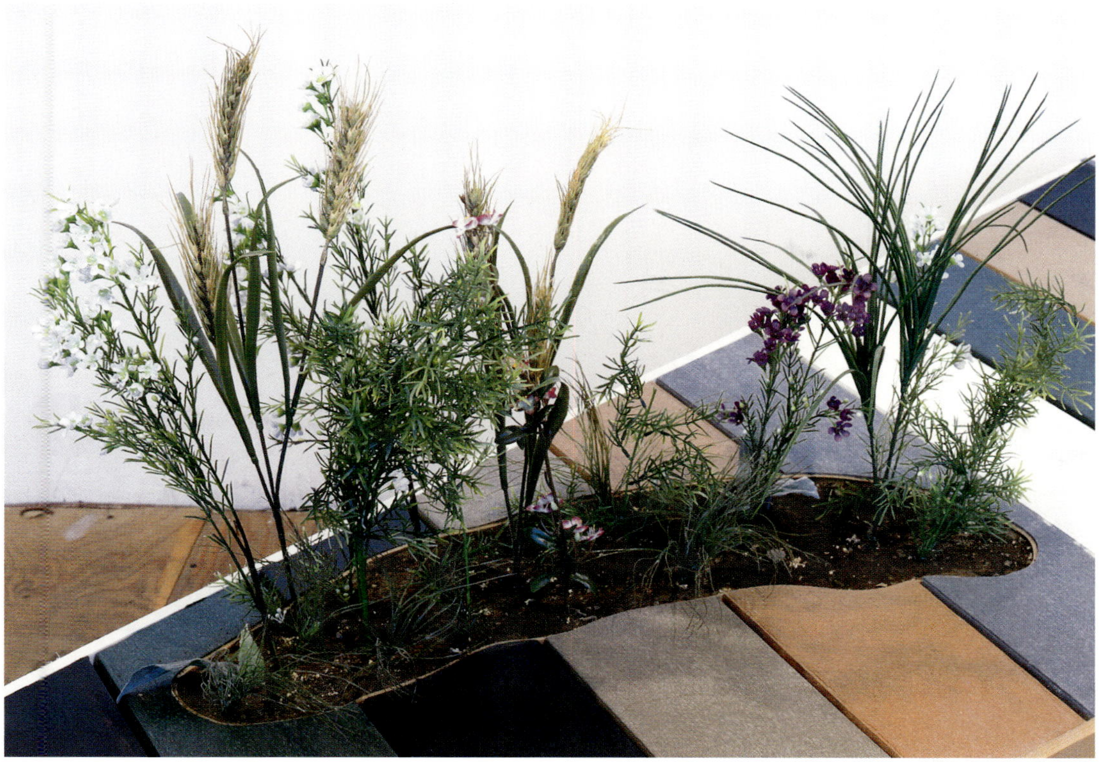

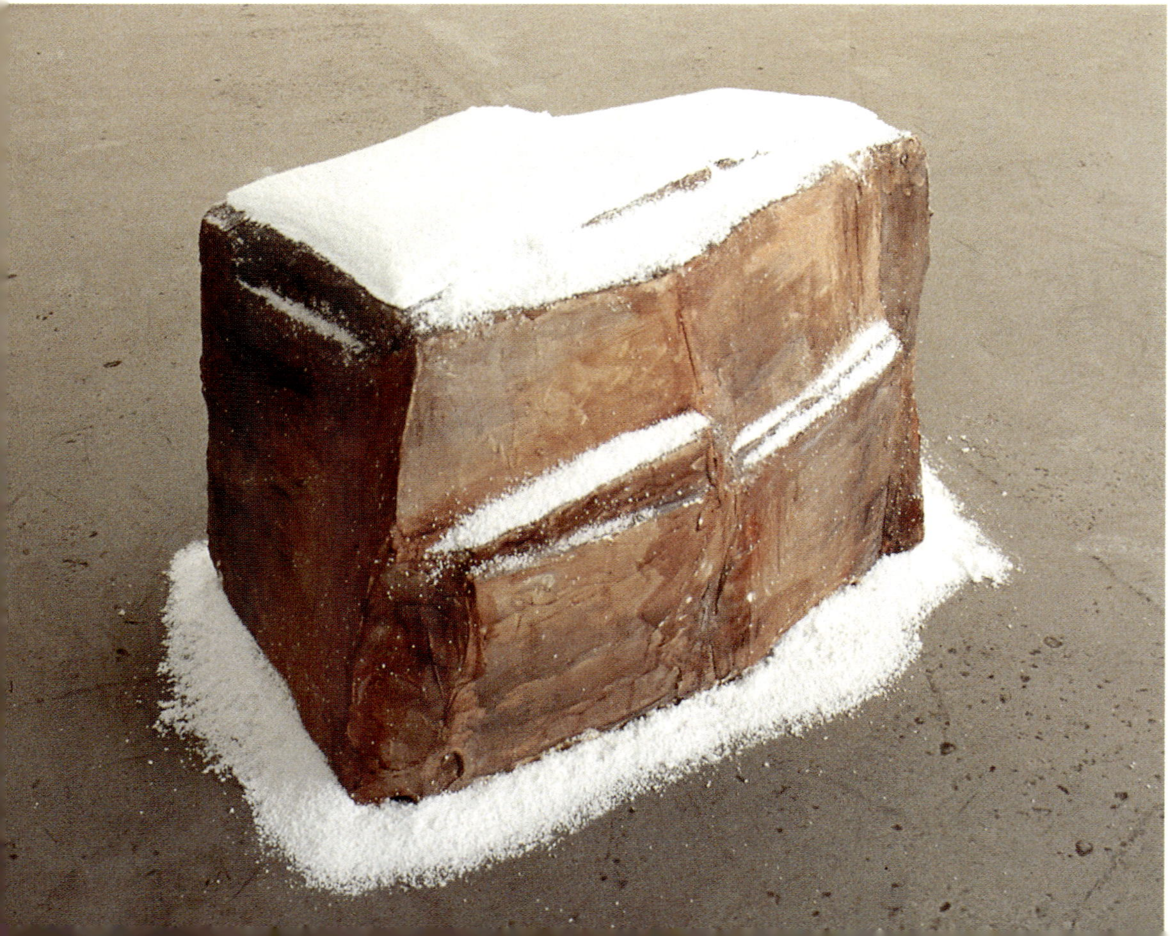

CLARA WILLIAMS

42. *Rock*, 2001

on facing page:
43. *Scout*, 2001

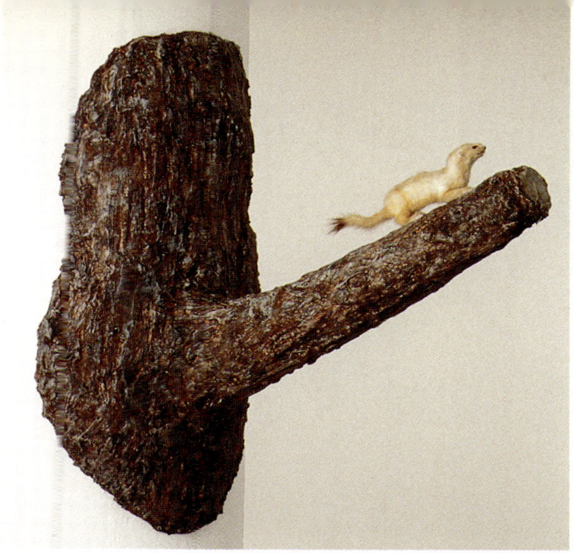



sculptor and a landscape designer, often makes work that conflates the ideas of taming nature for human indulgence and reinserting natural forms into pedestrian spaces. In *Plant* (cat. no. 17), made specifically for this exhibition, he presents a large-scale sculpture that doubles as a gallery bench and as an ordinary planter one might encounter in a typically impersonal corporate lobby. Sections of the bench, of various lengths, radiate out from a circular, planted center. The piece can be viewed as a sculpture or as a completely utilitarian object available for weary museum visitors to sit down on. The bench, with its deliberate design and colorful stripes, calls to mind a park bench—a haven from urban life, a place to commune with nature. However, if you sat on it you might feel as if you were sitting at ground level with weeds pushing up from beneath. Artificial plant fragments are strategically incorporated into the piece to give the illusion that real weeds and wildflowers are growing out of cracks in the bench.

Middlebrook understands the irony of the ever-expanding concrete environment having a direct effect on our longing for a natural paradise. He sees man's desire to control nature as evidence of our ultimate fear of nature. The plants that grow out of the bench are clues to what might lie underground, alluding to a pre-urban society characterized by unfettered growth. Middlebrook theorizes that the urban landscape acts as a skin, a constructed layer that merely sits on top of nature rather than annihilating it. In this scenario, things incessantly continue to grow, erode, and re-grow, changing all matter, including man-made objects. Seeing this work, you can imagine a future in which the natural realm stages a dramatic takeover of interior space, and the "white cube" gallery is no longer a pure, clean space free from the untamed elements of nature. Middlebrook humorously suggests that perhaps nature is really in control and that our attempts to hold back its progress are, in the end, futile.

Clara Williams also toys with the milieu of the gallery space in her installation *Scout* (cat. no. 43), in which a column that clearly serves no structural purpose stands in the gallery as though it might be part of the architecture. She uses the fabricated column as a stand-in for a tree, on which she has mounted a patch of bark with a protruding branch. An embalmed weasel is frozen in the act of scurrying up the branch, which abruptly ends in midair. Williams implies that the merest suggestion of a scene from nature is sufficient to evoke an entire pastoral narrative. By borrowing from the conventions of theatrical set design, natural-history dioramas, and zoos' fabricated animal habitats, she successfully brings the outdoors inside and involves the viewer in a fictional scenario.

Williams produced a more straightforward version of this effect in *Rock* (cat. no. 42), a hyperreal installation of an outcropping covered with Styrofoam "snow" that sits on the floor like a lost prop. Here, she playfully combines the romantic ideal of the great outdoors with the comically absurd setting of the cartoon “The Flintstones,” in which boulders serve as easy chairs and rooftops. Conjuring holiday decorations and department-store displays, the fake snow is a symbol of the widespread use of natural elements to sell products and ideas. Williams, who is interested in the visual joke that a replica plays on the viewer, creates illusions that are easily shattered by the viewer's knowledge of the difference between real and fake. Just as Eve's eating of the forbidden fruit from the tree of knowledge, and persuading Adam to do the same, robbed them of their innocence by making them aware of good and evil (and of their own nakedness), we cannot resist feasting our eyes on the artificiality that surrounds us, making us all the more aware of so much that is artificial in our lives.

*UnNaturally* brings together a variety of works that evoke a sense of awe and confusion about the environment in which we live. Meditations on authenticity and fakery, they lead us to call into question our understanding of the natural world and alienate us from the familiar. We begin to contemplate the ways in which our ever-evolving technological society has made the distinction between the real and the artificial harder and harder to discern, and yet ever more vital to preserve. This raises the troublesome question of simulated biology and the challenge it poses to our own relative importance.

Together, the works in the exhibition comprise a many-voiced commentary on the complex issue of real versus fake and an inquiry into the ways in which popular culture has become a major criterion in comparing the two. The artists whose work is featured here, with their tour-de-force craftsmanship and sardonic humor, raise provocative questions. Through their often satirical critiques of urban society's removal from the natural environment, they invite viewers to take part in an intelligent examination of the narrowing gap between nature and culture. The fabricated flowers, weeds, fungi, and other plant life on display remind us of the ubiquity of constructed environments in malls, zoos, and other themed "entertainment destinations" where nature has been tamed and packaged for consumer use. *UnNaturally* presents "new-and-improved" forms of nature that possess equal aesthetic value without the required maintenance and unpredictability of the natural world. We are left to question whether such "improvements" outweigh the benefits of living plants and unmediated experiences of nature and, furthermore, whether such experiences are even possible.

The ubiquitous physical and metaphorical artificiality we experience in daily life has come to define the way we understand the world. In the discourse of this exhibition, nature becomes a starting point for a much larger debate about the overuse of spectacle, simulacra, and "theme-ing" in everything from popular entertainment to urban planning. Perhaps the broader, more compelling issue at hand is how the Disney phenomenon and other forms of commercialized fantasy in contemporary culture have infringed on our experience of nature and our relationship to it.

Philip K. Dick

# PIPER IN THE WOODS

Well, Corporal Westerburg," Doctor Henry Harris said gently, "just why do you think you're a plant?"

As he spoke, Harris glanced down again at the card on his desk. It was from the Base Commander himself, made out in Cox's heavy scrawl:

DOC, THIS IS THE LAD I TOLD YOU ABOUT. TALK TO HIM AND TRY TO FIND OUT HOW HE GOT THIS DELUSION. HE'S FROM THE NEW GARRISON, THE NEW CHECK STATION ON ASTEROID Y-3, AND WE DON'T WANT ANYTHING TO GO WRONG THERE. ESPECIALLY A SILLY DAMN THING LIKE THIS!

Harris pushed the card aside and stared back up at the youth across the desk from him. The young man seemed ill at ease and appeared to be avoiding answering the question Harris had put to him. Harris frowned. Westerburg was a good looking chap, actually handsome in his patrol uniform, a shock of blond hair over one eye. He was tall, almost six feet, a fine healthy lad, just two years out of Training, according to the card. Born in Detroit. Had measles when he was nine. Interested in jet engines, tennis, and girls. Twenty-six years old.

"Well, Corporal Westerburg," Doctor Harris said again. "Why do you think you're a plant?"

The Corporal looked up shyly. He cleared his throat. "Sir, I AM a plant, I don't just think so. I've been a plant for several days now."

"I see." The Doctor nodded. "You mean that you weren't always a plant?"

"No sir. I just became a plant recently."

"And what were you before you became a plant?"

"Well, sir, I was just like the rest of you."

There was silence. Doctor Harris took up his pen and scratched a few lines, but nothing of importance came. A plant? And such a healthy-looking lad! Harris removed his steel-rimmed glasses and polished them with his handkerchief. He put them on again and leaned back in his chair. "Care for a cigarette, Corporal?"

"No, sir."

The doctor lit one for himself, resting his arm on the edge of the chair. "Corporal, you must realize that there are very few men who become plants, especially on such short notice. I have to admit you are the first person who has ever told me such a thing."

"Yes, sir, I realize it's quite rare."

"You can understand why I'm interested, then. When you say you're a plant, you mean you're not capable of mobility? Or do you mean you're a vegetable, as opposed to an animal? Or just what?"

The Corporal looked away. "I can't tell you anymore," he murmured. "I'm sorry, sir."

"Well, would you mind telling me how you became a plant?"



Corporal Westerburg hesitated. He stared down at the floor, then out the window at the spaceport, then at a fly on the desk. At last he stood up, getting slowly to his feet. "I can't even tell you that, sir," he said.

"You can't? Why not?"

"Because—because I promised not to."

The room was silent. Doctor Harris rose, too, and they both stood facing each other. Harris frowned, rubbing his jaw. "Corporal, just WHO did you promise?"

"I can't even tell you that, sir. I'm sorry."

The Doctor considered this. At last he went to the door and opened it. "All right, Corporal. You may go now. And thanks for your time."

"I'm sorry I'm not more helpful." The Corporal went slowly out and Harris closed the door after him. Then he went across his office to the vidphone. He rang Commander Cox's letter. A moment later the beefy good-natured face of the Base Commander appeared.

"Cox, this is Harris. I talked to him, all right. All I could get is the statement that he's a plant. What else it there? What kind of behavior pattern?"

"Well," Cox said, "the first thing they noticed was that he wouldn't do any work. The Garrison Chief reported that this Westerburg would wander off outside the Garrison and just sit, all day long. Just sit."

"In the sun?"

"Yes. Just sit in the sun. Then at nightfall he would come back in. When they asked why he wasn't working in the jet repair building he told them he had to be out in the sun. Then he said— Cox hesitated.

"Yes? Said what?"

"He said that work was unnatural. That it was a waste of time. That the only worthwhile thing was to sit and contemplate—outside."

"What then?"

"Then they asked him how he got that idea, and then he revealed to them that he had become a plant."

"I'm going to have to talk to him again, I can see," Harris said. "And he's applied for a permanent discharge from the Patrol? What reason did he give?"

"The same, that he's a plant now, and has no more interest in being a Patrolman. All he wants to do is sit in the sun. It's the damnedest thing I ever heard."

"All right. I think I'll visit him in his quarters." Harris looked at his watch. "I'll go over after dinner."

"Good luck," Cox said gloomily. "But who ever heard of a man turning into a plant? We told him it wasn't possible, but he just smiled at us."

"I'll let you know how I make out," Harris said.



Harris walked slowly down the hall. It was after six; the evening meal was over. A dim concept was coming into his mind, but it was much too soon to be sure. He increased his pace, turning right at the end of the hall. Two nurses passed, hurrying by. Westerburg was quartered with a buddy, a man who had been injured in a jet blast and who was now almost recovered. Harris came to the dorm wing and stopped, checking the numbers on the doors.

"Can I help you, sir?" the robot attendant said, gliding up.

"I'm looking for Corporal Westerburg's room."

"Three doors to the right."

Harris went on. Asteroid Y–3 had only recently been garrisoned and staffed. It had become the primary check-point to halt and examine ships entering the system from outer-space. The Garrison made sure that no dangerous bacteria, fungus, or what-not arrived to infect the system. A nice asteroid it was, warm, well-watered, with trees and lakes and lots of sunshine. And the most modern Garrison in the nine planets. He shook his head, coming to the third door. He stopped, raising his hand and knocking.

"Who's there?" sounded through the door.

"I want to see Corporal Westerburg."

The door opened. A bovine youth with horn-rimmed glasses looked out, a book in his hand. "Who are you?"

"Doctor Harris."

"I'm sorry, sir. Corporal Westerburg is asleep."

"Would he mind if I woke him up? I want very much to talk to him." Harris peered inside. He could see a neat room, with a desk, a rug, and a lamp, and two bunks. On one of the bunks was Westerburg, lying face up, his arms folded across his chest, his eyes tightly closed.

"Sir," the bovine youth said, "I'm afraid I can't wake him up for you, much as I'd like to."

"You can't? Why not?"

"Sir, Corporal Westerburg won't wake up, not after the sun sets. He just won't. He can't be wakened."

"Cataleptic? Really?"

"But in the morning, as soon as the sun comes up, he leaps out of bed and goes outside. Stays the whole day."

"I see," the Doctor said." Well, thanks anyhow." He went back out into the hall and the door shut after him. "There's more to this than I realized," he murmured. He went on back the way he had come.

It was a warm sunny day. The sky was almost free of clouds and a gentle wind moved through the cedars along the bank of the stream. There was a path leading from the hospital building down the slope to the stream. At the stream a small bridge led over to the other side, and a few patients were standing on the bridge, wrapped in their bathrobes, looking aimlessly down at the water.

It took Harris several minutes to find Westerburg. The youth was not with the other patients, near or around the bridge. He had gone farther down, past the cedar trees and out onto a strip of bright meadow, where poppies and grass grew everywhere. He was sitting on the stream bank, on a flat gray stone, leaning back and staring up, his mouth open a little. He did not notice the Doctor until Harris was almost beside him.



"Hello," Harris said softly.

Westerburg opened his eyes, looking up. He smiled and got slowly to his feet, a graceful, flowing motion that was rather surprising for a man of his size. "Hello, Doctor. What brings you out here?"

"Nothing. Thought I'd get some sun."

"Here, you can share my rock," Westerburg moved over and Harris sat down gingerly, being careful not to touch his trousers on the sharp edges of the rock. He lit a cigarette and gazed silently down at the water. Beside him, Westerburg had resumed his strange position, leaning back, resting on his hands, staring up with his eyes shut tight.

"Nice day," the Doctor said.

"Yes."

"Do you come here every day?"

"You like it better out here than inside."

"I can't stay inside," Westerburg said.

"You can't? How do you mean, 'can't'?"

"You would die without AIR, wouldn't you?" the Corporal said.

"And you'd die without sunlight?"

Westerburg nodded.

"Corporal, may I ask you something? Do you plan to do this for the rest of your life, sit out in the sun on a flat rock? Nothing else?"

Westerburg nodded.

"How about your job? You went to school for years to become a Patrolman. You wanted to enter the Patrol very badly. You were given a fine rating and a first-class position. How do you feel, giving that all up? You know, it won't be easy to get back in again. Do you realize that?"

"I realize it."

"And you're really going to give it all up?"

"That's right."

Harris was silent for a while. At last he put his cigarette out and turned toward the youth. "All right, let's say you give up your job and sit in the sun. Well, what happens, then? Someone else has to do the job instead of you. Isn't that true? The job has to be done, YOUR job has to be done. And if you don't do it someone else has to."

"I suppose so."

"Westerburg, suppose everyone felt the way you do? Suppose everyone wanted to sit in the sun all day? What would happen? No one would check ships coming from outer space. Bacteria and toxic crystals would enter the system and cause mass death and suffering. Isn't that right?"



"If everyone felt the way I do they wouldn't be going into outer space."

"But they have to. They have to trade, they have to get minerals and products and new plants."

"Why?"

"To keep society going."

"Why?"

"Well—" Harris gestured. "People couldn't live without society."

Westerburg said nothing to that. Harris watched him, but the youth did not answer.

"Isn't that right?" Harris said.

"Perhaps. It's a peculiar business, Doctor. You know, I struggled for years to get through Training. I had to work and pay my own way. Washed dishes, worked in kitchens. Studied at night, learned, crammed, worked on and on. And you know what I think, now?"

"What?"

"I wish I'd become a plant earlier."

Doctor Harris stood up. "Westerburg, when you come inside, will you stop off at my office? I want to give you a few tests, if you don't mind."

"The shock box?" Westerburg smiled. "I knew that would be coming around. Sure, I don't mind."

Nettled, Harris left the rock, walking back up the bank a short distance. "About three, Corporal?"

The Corporal nodded.

Harris made his way up the hill, to the path, toward the hospital building. The whole thing was beginning to become more clear to him. A boy who had struggled all his life. Financial insecurity. Idealized goal, getting a Patrol assignment. Finally reached it, found the load too great. And on Asteroid Y–3 there was too much vegetation to look at all day. Primitive identification and projection on the flora of the asteroid. Concept of security involved in immobility and permanence. Unchanging forest.

He entered the building. A robot orderly stopped him almost at once. "Sir, Commander Cox wants you urgently, on the vidphone."

"Thanks." Harris strode to the office. He dialed Cox's letter and the Commander's face came presently into focus. "Cox? This is Harris. I've been out talking to the boy. I'm beginning to get this lined up, now. I can see the pattern, too much load too long. Finally gets what he wants and the idealization shatters under the—"

"Harris!" Cox barked. "Shut up and listen. I just got a report from Y–3. They're sending an express rocket here. It's on the way."

"An express rocket?"

"Five more cases like Westerburg. All say they're plants! The Garrison Chief is worried as hell. Says we MUST find out what it is or the Garrison will fall apart, right away. Do you get me, Harris? Find out what it is!"

"Yes, sir," Harris murmured. "Yes, sir."

By the end of the week there were twenty cases, and all, of course, were from Asteroid Y–3.

Commander Cox and Harris stood together at the top of the hill, looking gloomily down at the stream below. Sixteen men and four women sat in the sun along the bank, none of them moving, none speaking. An hour had gone by since Cox and Harris appeared, and in all that time the twenty people below had not stirred.

"I don't get it," Cox said, shaking his head. "I just absolutely don't get it. Harris, is this the beginning of the end? Is everything going to start cracking around us? It gives me a hell of a strange feeling to see those people down there basking away in the sun, just sitting and basking."

"Who's that man there with the red hair?"

"That's Ulrich Deutsch. He was Second in Command at the Garrison. Now look at him! Sits and dozes with his mouth open and his eyes shut. A week ago that man was climbing, going right up to the top. When the Garrison Chief retires he was supposed to take over. Maybe another year, at the most. All his life he's been climbing to get up there."

"And now he sits in the sun," Harris finished.

"That woman. The brunette, with the short hair. Career woman. Head of the entire office staff at the Garrison. And the man beside her. Janitor. And that cute little gal there, with the bosom. Secretary, just out of school. All kinds. And I got a note this morning, three more coming in sometime today."

Harris nodded. "The strange thing is—they really WANT to sit down there. They're completely rational; they could do something else, but they just don't care to."

"Well?" Cox said. "What are you going to do? Have you found anything? We're counting on you. Let's hear it."

"I couldn't get anything out of them directly," Harris said, "but I've had some interesting results with the shock box. Let's go inside and I'll show you."

"Fine," Cox turned and started toward the hospital. "Show me anything you've got. This is serious. Now I know how Tiberius felt when Christianity showed up in high places."

Harris snapped off the light. The room was pitch black. "I'll run this first reel for you. The subject is one of the best biologists stationed at the Garrison. Robert Bradshaw. He came in yesterday. I got a good run from the shock box because Bradshaw's mind is so highly differentiated. There's a lot of repressed material of a non-rational nature, more than usual."

He pressed a switch. The projector whirred, and on the far wall a three-dimensional image appeared in color, so real that it might have been the man himself. Robert Bradshaw was a man of fifty, heavy-set, with iron-gray hair and a square jaw. He sat in the chair calmly, his hands resting on the arms, oblivious to the electrodes attached to his neck and wrist. "There I go," Harris said. "Watch."



His film-image appeared, approaching Bradshaw. "Now, Mr. Bradshaw," his image said, "this won't hurt you at all, and it'll help us a lot." The image rotated the controls on the shock box, Bradshaw stiffened, and his jaw set, but otherwise he gave no sign. The image of Harris regarded him for a time and then stepped away from the controls.

"Can you hear me, Mr. Bradshaw?" the image asked.

"Yes."

"What is your name?"

"Robert C. Bradshaw."

"What is your position?"

"Chief Biologist at the check station on Y—3."

"Are you there now?"

"No, I'm back on Terra. In a hospital."

"Why?"

"Because I admitted to the Garrison Chief that I had become a plant."

"Is that true? That you are a plant?"

"Yes, in a non-biological sense. I retain the physiology of a human being, of course."

"What do you mean, then, that you're a plant?"

"The reference is to attitudinal response, to Weltanschauung."

"Go on."

"It is possible for a warm-blooded animal, an upper primate, to adopt the psychology of a plant, to some extent."

"Yes?"

"I refer to this."

"And the others? They refer to this also?"

"Yes."

"How did this occur, your adopting this attitude?"

Bradshaw's image hesitated, the lips twisting. "See?" Harris said to Cox. "Strong conflict. He wouldn't have gone on, if he had only been fully conscious."

"I—"

"Yes?"

"I was taught to become a plant."

The image of Harris showed surprise and interest. "What do you mean, you were taught to become a plant?"

"They realized my problems and taught me to become a plant. Now I'm free from them, the problems."

"Who? Who taught you?"

"The Pipers."

"Who? The Pipers? Who are the Pipers?"

There was no answer.

"Mr. Bradshaw, who are the Pipers?"

After a long, agonized pause, the heavy lips parted. "They live in the woods . . ."

Harris snapped off the projector, and the lights came on. He and Cox blinked. "That was all I could get," Harris said. "But I was lucky to get that. He wasn't supposed to tell, not at all. That was the thing they all promised not to do, tell who taught them to become plants. The Pipers who live in the woods on Asteroid Y–3."

"You got this story from all twenty?"

"No." Harris grimaced. "Most of them put up too much fight. I couldn't even get this much from them."

Cox reflected. "The Pipers. Well? What do you propose to do? Just wait around until you can get the full story? Is that your program?"

"No." Harris said. "Not at all. I'm going to Y–3 and find out who the Pipers are, myself."

The small patrol ship made its landing with care and precision, its jets choking into final silence. The hatch slid back and Doctor Henry Harris found himself staring out at a field, a brown, sun-baked landing field. At the end of the field was a tall signal tower. Around the field on all sides were long gray buildings, the Garrison check station itself. Not far off a huge Venusian cruiser was parked, a vast green hulk, like an enormous lime. The technicians from the station were swarming all over it, checking and examining each inch of it for lethal life-forms and poisons that might have attached themselves to the hull.

"All out, sir," the pilot said.

Harris nodded. He took hold of his two suitcases and stepped carefully down. The ground was hot underfoot, and he blinked in the bright sunlight. Jupiter was in the sky, and the vast planet reflected considerable sunlight down onto the asteroid.

Harris started across the field, carrying his suitcase. A field attendant was already busy opening the storage compartment of the Patrol ship, extracting his trunk. The attendant lowered the trunk into a waiting dolly and came after him, manipulating the little truck with bored skill.

As Harris came to the entrance of the signal tower the gate slid back and a man came forward, an older man, large and robust, with white hair and a steady walk.

"How are you, Doctor?" he said, holding his hand out. "I'm Lawrence Watts, the Garrison Chief."

They shook hands. Watts smiled down at Harris. He was a huge old man, still regal and straight in his dark blue uniform, with his gold epaulets sparkling on his shoulders.



"Have a good trip?" Watts asked. "Come on inside and I'll have a drink fixed for you. It gets hot around here, with the Big Mirror up there."

"Jupiter?" Harris followed him inside the building. The signal tower was cool and dark, a welcome relief. "Why is the gravity so near Terra's? I expected to go flying off like a kangaroo. Is it artificial?"

"No. There's a dense core of some kind to the asteroid, some kind of metallic deposit. That's why we picked this asteroid out of all the others. It made the construction problem much simpler, and it also explains why the asteroid has natural air and water. Did you see the hills?"

"The hills?"

"When we get up higher in the tower we'll be able to see over the buildings. There's quite a natural park here, a regular little forest, complete with everything you'd want. Come in here, Harris. This is my office." The old man strode at quite a clip, around the corner and into a large, well-furnished apartment. "Isn't this pleasant? I intend to make my last year here as amiable as possible." He frowned. "Off course, with Deutsch gone, I may be here forever. Oh, well." He shrugged. "Sit down, Harris."

"Thanks." Harris took a chair, stretching his legs out. He watched Watts as he closed the door to the hall. "By the way, any more cases come up?"

"Two more today." Watts was grim. "Makes almost thirty, in all. We have three hundred men in this station. At the rate it's going—"

"Chief, you spoke about a forest on the asteroid. Do you allow the crew to go into the forest at will? Or do you restrict them to the buildings and grounds?"

Watts rubbed his jaw. "Well, it's a difficult situation, Harris. I have to let the men leave the grounds sometimes. They can SEE the forest from the buildings, and as long as you can see a nice place to stretch out and relax that does it. Once every ten days they have a full period of rest. Then they go out and fool around."

"And then it happens?"

"Yes, I suppose so. But as long as they can see the forest, they'll want to go. I can't help it."

"I know. I'm not censuring you. Well, what's your theory? What happens to them out there? What do the do?"

"What happens? Once they get out there and take it easy for a while they don't want to come back and work. It's boondoggling. Playing hookey. They don't want to work, so off they go."

"How about this business of their delusions?"

Watts laughed good-naturedly. "Listen, Harris. You know as well as I do that's a lot of poppycock. They're no more plants than you or I. They just don't want to work, that's all. When I was a cadet we had a few ways to make people work. I wish I could lay a few on their backs, like we used to."

"You think this is simple goldbricking, then?"

"Don't you think it is?"

"No," Harris said. "They really believe they're plants. I put them through the high-frequency shock treatment, the shock box. The whole nervous system is paralyzed, all inhibitions stopped cold. They tell the truth, then. And they said the same thing—and more."



Watts paced back and forth, his hands clasped behind his back. "Harris, you're a doctor, and I suppose you know what you're talking about. But look at the situation here. We have a garrison, a good modern garrison. We're probably the most modern outfit in the system. Every new device and gadget is here that science can produce. Harris, this garrison is one vast machine. The men are parts, and each has his job, the Maintenance Crew, the Biologists, the Office Crew, the Managerial Staff.

"Look what happens when one person steps away from his job. Everything else begins to creak. We can't service the bugs if no one services the machines. We can't order food to feed the crews if no one makes out reports, takes inventories. We can't direct any kind of activity if the Second in Command decides to go out and sit in the sun all day.

"Thirty people, one tenth of the Garrison. But we can't run without them. The Garrison is built that way. If you take the supports out the whole building falls. No one can leave. We're all tied here and these people know it. They know they have no right to do that, run off on their own. No one has that right anymore. We're all too tightly interwoven to suddenly start doing what we want. It's unfair to the rest, the majority."

Harris nodded. "Chief, can I ask you something?"

"What is it?"

"Are there any inhabitants on the asteroid? Any natives?"

"Natives?" Watts considered. "Yes, there's some kind of aborigines living out there." He waved vaguely toward the window.

"What are they like? Have you seen them?"

"Yes, I've seen them. At least, I saw them when we first came here. They hung around for a while, watching us, then after a time they disappeared."

"Did they die off? Diseases of some kind?"

"No. They just—just disappeared. Into their forest. They're still there, someplace."

“What kind of people are they?”

“Well, the story is that they’re originally from Mars. They don’t look much like Martians, though. They’re dark, a kind of coppery color. Thin. Very agile, in their own way. They hunt and fish. No written language. We don’t pay much attention to them.”

“I see.” Harris paused. “Chief, have you ever heard of anything called—the Pipers?”

“The Pipers?” Watts frowned. “No. Why?”

“The patients mentioned something called the Pipers. According to Bradshaw, the Pipers taught him to become a plant. He learned it from them, a kind of teaching.”

“The Pipers. What are they?”

“I don’t know,” Harris admitted. “I thought maybe you might know. My first assumption, of course, was that they’re the natives. But now I’m not so sure, after hearing your description of them.”



“The natives are primitive savages. They don’t have anything to teach anybody, especially a top-flight biologist.”

Harris hesitated. “Chief, I’d like to go into the woods and look around. Is that possible?”

“Certainly. I can arrange it for you. I’ll give you one of the men to show you around.”

“I’d rather go alone. Is there any danger?”

“No, none that I know of. Except—”

“Except the Pipers,” Harris finished. “I know. Well, there’s only one way to find them, and that’s it. I’ll have to take my chances.”

“If you walk in a straight line,” Chief Watts said, “you’ll find yourself back at the Garrison in about six hours. It’s a damn small asteroid. There’s a couple of streams and lakes, so don’t fall in.”

“How about snakes or poisonous insects?”

“Nothing like that reported. We did a lot of tramping around at first, but it’s grown back now, the way it was. We never encountered anything dangerous.”

“Thanks, Chief,” Harris said. They shook hands. “I’ll see you before nightfall.”

“Good luck.” The Chief and his two armed escorts turned and went back across the rise, down the other side toward the Garrison. Harris watched them go until they disappeared inside the building. Then he turned and started into the grove of trees.

The woods were very silent around him as he walked. Trees towered up on all sides of him, huge dark-green trees like eucalyptus. The ground underfoot was soft with endless leaves that had fallen and rotted into the soil. After awhile the grove of high trees fell behind and he found himself crossing a dry meadow, the grass and weeds burned brown in the sun. Insects buzzed around him, rising up from the dry weed-stalks. Something scuttled ahead, hurrying through the undergrowth. He caught sight of a gray ball with many legs, scampering furiously, its antennae weaving.

The meadow ended at the bottom of a hill. He was going up, now, going higher and higher. Ahead of him an endless expanse of green rose, acres of wild growth. He scrambled to the top finally, blowing and panting, catching his breath.

He went on. Now he was going down again, plunging into a deep gully. Tall ferms grew, as large as trees. He was entering a living Jurassic forest, ferns that stretched out endlessly ahead of him. Down he went, walking carefully. The air began to turn cold around him. The floor of the gully was damp and silent; underfoot the ground was almost wet.

He came out on a level table. It was dark, with the ferns growing up on all sides, dense growths of ferns, silent and unmoving. He came upon a natural path, an old stream bed, rough and rocky, but easy to follow. The air was thick and oppressive. Beyond the ferns he could see the side of the next hill, a green field rising up.

Something gray was ahead. Rocks, piled-up boulders, scattered and stacked here and there. The stream led directly to them. Apparently this had been a pool of some kind, a stream emptying from it. He climbed the first of the boulders awkwardly, feeling his way up. At the top he paused, resting again.

As yet he had had no luck. So far he had not met any of the natives. It would be through them that he would find the mysterious Pipers that were stealing the men away, if such really existed. If he could find the natives, talk to them, perhaps he could find out something. But as yet he had been unsuccessful. He looked around. The woods were very silent. A slight breeze moved through the ferns rustling them, but that was all. Where were the natives? Probably they had a settlement of some sort, huts, a clearing. The asteroid was small, he should be able to find them by nightfall.

He started down the rocks. More rocks rose up ahead and he climbed them. Suddenly he stopped, listening. Far off, he could hear a sound, the sound of water. Was he approaching a pool of some kind? He went on again, trying to locate the sound. He scrambled down rocks and up rocks, and all around him there was silence, except for the splashing of distant water. Maybe a waterfall, water in motion. A stream. If he found the stream he might find the natives.

The rocks ended and the stream bed began again, but this time it was wet, the bottom muddy and overgrown with moss. He was on the right track; not too long ago this stream had flowed, probably during the rainy season. He went up on the side of the stream, pushing through the ferns and vines. A golden snake slid expertly out of his path. Something glinted ahead, something sparkling through the ferns. Water. A pool. He hurried, pushing the vines aside and stepping out, leaving them behind.

He was standing on the edge of a pool, a deep pool sunk in a hollow of gray rocks, surrounded by ferns and vines. The water was clear and bright, and in motion, flowing in a waterfall at the far end. It was beautiful, and he stood watching, marveling at it, the undisturbed quality of it. Untouched, it was. Just as it had always been, probably. As long as the asteroid existed. Was he the first to see it? Perhaps. It was so hidden, so concealed by the ferns. It gave him a strange feeling, a feeling almost of ownership. He stepped down a little toward the water.

And it was then he noticed her.

The girl was sitting on the far edge of the pool, staring down into the water, resting her head on one drawn-up knee. She had been bathing; he could see that at once. Her coppery body was still wet and glistening with moisture, sparkling in the sun. She had not seen him. He stopped, holding his breath, watching her.

She was lovely, very lovely, with long dark hair that wound around her shoulders and arms. Her body was slim, very slender, with a supple grace to it that made him stare, accustomed as he was to various forms of anatomy. How silent she was! Silent and unmoving, staring down at the water. Time passed, strange, unchanging time, as he watched the girl. Time might even have ceased, with the girl sitting on the rock staring into the water, and the rows of great ferns behind her, as rigid as if they had been painted there.



All at once the girl looked up. Harris shifted, suddenly conscious of himself as an intruder. He stepped back. "I'm sorry," he murmured. "I'm from the Garrison. I didn't mean to come poking around."

She nodded without speaking.

"You don't mind?" Harris asked presently.

"No."

So she spoke Terran! He moved a little toward her, around the side of the pool. "I hope you don't mind my bothering you. I won't be on the asteroid very long. This is my first day here. I just arrived from Terra."

She smiled faintly.

"I'm a doctor. Henry Harris." He looked down at her, at the slim coppery body gleaming in the sunlight, a faint sheen of moisture on her arms and thighs. "You might be interested in why I'm here." He paused. "Maybe you can even help me."

She looked up a little. "Oh?"

"Would you like to help me?"

She smiled. "Yes. Of course."

"That's good. Mind if I sit down?" He looked around and found himself a flat rock. He sat down slowly, facing her. "Cigarette?"

"No."

"Well, I'll have one." He lit up, taking a deep breath. "You see, we have a problem at the Garrison. Something has been happening to some of the men, and it seems to be spreading. We have to find out what causes it or we won't be able to run the Garrison."

He waited for a moment. She nodded slightly. How silent she was! Silent and unmoving. Like the ferns.

"Well, I've been able to find out a few things from them, and one very interesting fact stands out. They keep saying that something called—called the Pipers are responsible for their condition. They say the Pipers taught them—" He stopped. A strange look had flittered across her dark, small face. "Do you know the Pipers?"

She nodded.

Acute satisfaction flooded over Harris. "You do? I was sure the natives would know." He stood up again. "I was sure they would, if the Pipers really existed. They do exist, do they?"

"They exist."

Harris frowned. "And they're here, in the woods?"

"Yes."

"I see." He ground his cigarette out impatiently. "You don't suppose there's any chance you could take me to them, do you?"

"Take you?"

"Yes. I have this problem and I have to solve it. You see, the Base Commander on Terra has assigned this to me, this business about the Pipers. It has to be solved. And I'm the one assigned to the job. So it's important to me to find them. Do you see? Do you understand?"

She nodded.

"Well, will you take me to them?"

The girl was silent. For a long time she sat, staring down at the water, resting her head against her knee. Harris began to become impatient. He fidgeted back and forth, resting first on one leg and then on the other.

"Well, will you?" he said again. "It's important to the whole Garrison. What do you say?" He felt around his pockets. "Maybe I could give you something. What do I have . . ." He brought out his lighter. "I could give you my lighter."

The girl stood up, rising slowly, gracefully, without motion or effort. Harris' mouth fell open. How supple she was, gliding to her feet in a single motion! He blinked. Without effort she had stood, seemingly without CHANGE. All at once she was standing instead of sitting, standing and looking calmly at him, her small face expressionless.

"Will you?" he said.

"Yes. Come along." She turned away, moving toward the row of ferns.

Harris followed quickly, stumbling across the rocks. "Fine," he said. "Thanks a lot. I'm very interested to meet these Pipers. Where are you taking me, to your village? How much time do we have before nightfall?"

The girl did not answer. She had entered the ferns already, and Harris quickened his pace to keep from losing her. How silently she glided!

"Wait," he called. "Wait for me."

The girl paused, waiting for him, slim and lovely, looking silently back. He entered the ferns, hurrying after her.

Well I'll be damned!" Commander Cox said. "It sure didn't take you long." He leaped down the steps two at a time. "Let me give you a hand."

Harris grinned, lugging his heavy suitcases. He set them down and breathed a sigh of relief. "It isn't worth it," he said. "I'm going to give up taking so much."

"Come on inside. Soldier, give him a hand." A Patrolman hurried over and took one of the suitcases. The three men went inside and down the corridor to Harris' quarters. Harris unlocked the door and the Patrolman deposited his suitcase inside.

"Thanks," Harris said. He set the other down beside it. "It's good to be back, even for a little while."

"A little while?"

"I just came back to settle my affairs. I have to return to Y–3 tomorrow morning."

"Then you didn't solve the problem?"

"I solved it, but I haven't CURED it. I'm going back and get to work right away. There's a lot to be done."

"But you found out what it is?"



"Yes. It was just what the men said. The Pipers."

"The Pipers do exist?"

"Yes." Harris nodded. "They do exist." He removed his coat and put it over the back of the chair. Then he went to the window and let it down. Warm spring air rushed into the room. He settled himself on the bed, leaning back.

"The Pipers exist, all right—in the minds of the Garrison crew! To the crew, the Pipers are real. The crew created them. It's a mass hypnosis, a group projection, all the men there have it, to some degree."

"How did it start?"

"Those men on Y–3 were sent because they were skilled, highly-trained men with exceptional ability. All their lives they've been schooled by complex modern society, fast tempo and high integration between people. Constant pressure toward some goal, some job to be done.

"Those men are put down suddenly on an asteroid where there are natives living the most primitive of existence, completely vegetable lives. No concept of goal, no concept of purpose, and hence no ability to plan. The natives live the way the animals live, from day to day, sleeping, picking food from the trees. A kind of Garden-of-Eden existence, without struggle or conflict."

"So? But—"

"Each of the Garrison crew sees the natives and UNCONSCIOUSLY thinks of his own early life, when he was a child, when HE had no worries, no responsibilities, before he joined modern society. A baby lying in the sun.

"But he can't admit this to himself! He can't admit that he might WANT to live like the natives, to lie and sleep all day. So he invents the Pipers, the idea of a mysterious group living in the woods who trap him, lead him into their kind of life. Then he can blame THEM, not himself. They 'teach' him to become a part of the woods."

"What are you going to do? Have the woods burned?"

"No." Harris shook his head. "That's not the answer; the woods are harmless. The answer is psycho-therapy for the men. That's why I'm going right back, so I can begin work. They've got to be made to see that the Pipers are inside them, their own unconscious voices calling to them to give up their responsibilities. They've got to be made to realize that here are no Pipers, at least, not outside themselves. The woods are harmless and the natives have nothing to teach anyone. They're primitive savages, without even a written language. We're seeing a psychological projection by a whole Garrison of men who want to lay down their work and take it easy for a while."

The room was silent.

"I see," Cox said presently. "Well, it makes sense." He got to his feet. "I hope you can do something with the men you get back."

"I hope so, too," Harris agreed. "And I think I can. After all, it's just a question of increasing their self-awareness. When they have that the Pipers will vanish."



Cox nodded. "Well, you go ahead with your unpacking, Doc. I'll see you at dinner. And maybe before you leave, tomorrow."

"Fine."

Harris opened the door and the Commander went out into the hall. Harris closed the door after him and then went back across the room. He looked out the window for a moment, his hands in his pockets.

It was becoming evening, the air was turning cool. The sun was just setting as he watched, disappearing behind the buildings of the city surrounding the hospital. He watched it go down.

Then he went over to his two suitcases. He was tired, very tired from his trip. A great weariness was beginning to descend over him. There were so many things to do, so terribly many. How could he hope to do them all? Back to the asteroid. And then what?"

He yawned, his eyes closing. How sleepy he was! He looked over at the bed. Then he sat down on the edge of it and took his shoes off. So much to do, the next day.

He put his shoes in the corner of the room. Then he bent over, unsnapping one of the suitcases. He opened the suitcase. From it he took a bulging gunny-sack. Carefully, he emptied the contents of the sack out on the floor. Dirt, rich soft dirt. Dirt he had collected during his last hours there, dirt he had carefully gathered up.

When the dirt was spread out on the floor he sat down in the middle of it. He stretched himself out, leaning back. When he was fully comfortable he folded his hands across his chest and closed his eyes. So much work to do— But later on, of course. Tomorrow. How warm the dirt was . . .

He was sound asleep in a moment.

# *Exhibition Checklist*

*Note: height precedes width precedes depth*



CHRIS ASTLEY

1. *Volume IV*, 2000
   C-print
   35¾ x 59¾ in. (91 x 152 cm)
   Courtesy of the artist
   (p. 28)

2. *Volume V*, 2000
   C-print
   35¾ x 59¾ in. (91 x 152 cm)
   Collection of Michael Formica and Bob Heimstra

3. *Volume VI*, 2000
   C-print
   19 x 29¾ in. (48 x 76 cm)
   Collection of Michael Formica and Bob Heimstra
   (pp. 3, 29)

GREGORY CREWDSON

4. *Untitled (Bedroom Tree)*, 2001
   from the *Twilight* series
   Digital C-print
   48 x 60 in. (122 x 152 cm)
   Collection of Ruth and Jake Bloom, Sun Valley, Idaho, courtesy Fine Art and Collectibles, Los Angeles, California

5. *Untitled (Flower Beanstalk)*, 2001
   from the *Twilight* series
   Digital C-print
   48 x 60 in. (122 x 152 cm)
   Collection of Ruth and Jake Bloom, Sun Valley, Idaho, courtesy Fine Art and Collectibles, Los Angeles, California
   (p. 27)

6. *Untitled (Flower Pile)*, 2001
   from the *Twilight* series
   Digital C-print
   48 x 60 in. (122 x 152 cm)
   Collection of Ruth and Jake Bloom, Sun Valley, Idaho, courtesy Fine Art and Collectibles, Los Angeles, California
   (p. 26)

JACCI DEN HARTOG

7. *Passing a Pleasant Summer II*, 1999
   Polyurethane, Hydrocal, and steel
   22 x 9½ x 18 in. (56 x 24 x 46 cm)
   Courtesy of the artist and Christopher Grimes Gallery, Santa Monica, California

8. *Traveling with My Heart Above My Head*, 1997
   Polyurethane, Hydrocal, and steel
   25 x 22 x 19 in. (63 x 56 x 48 cm)
   Courtesy of the artist and Christopher Grimes Gallery, Santa Monica, California
   (p. 34)

9. *Garden for Walking Through Water*, 1999
   Polyurethane, Hydrocal, and steel
   55 x 29 x 31 in. (140 x 74 x 79 cm)
   Courtesy of the artist and Christopher Grimes Gallery, Santa Monica, California
   (pp. 2, 35)

ALLAN DESOUZA

10. *Terrain #1*, 1999–2000
    C-print
    12 x 18 in. (30 x 46 cm)
    Courtesy of the artist

11. *Terrain #3*, 1999–2000
    C-print
    12 x 18 in. (30 x 46 cm)
    Courtesy of the artist

12. *Terrain #5*, 1999–2000
    C-print
    12 x 18 in. (30 x 46 cm)
    Courtesy of the artist
    (p. 30)

13. *Terrain #7*, 1999–2000
    C-print
    12 x 18 in. (30 x 46 cm)
    Courtesy of the artist
    (pp. 4, 30)

14. *Terrain #8*, 1999–2000
    C-print
    12 x 18 in. (30 x 46 cm)
    Courtesy of the artist
    (p. 31)

KEITH EDMIER

15. *Keith's Paphiopedilum (Version One)*, 2001
    Acrylic paint on dental acrylic
    3 x 4 x 10 in. (8 x 10 x 25 cm)
    Courtesy Friedrich Petzel Gallery, New York
    (p. 22)

### IÑIGO MANGLANO-OVALLE

16. *Sonambulo*, 1996–98 *
    Compact disc and two speakers
    Dimensions variable
    Courtesy of the artist and Max Protetch Gallery, New York
    * *Sonambulo*, originally created as a sound-and-light installation, is presented in this exhibition as a sound installation.
    (p. 19)

### JASON MIDDLEBROOK

17. *Plant*, 2002
    Plastic, lumber, silk plants, and paint
    Each bench: 15 x 36 x 84 in. (38 x 91 x 213 cm)
    Courtesy of the artist and Sara Meltzer Gallery, New York
    (pp. 44–45)

### NICOLETTA MUNROE

18. *Cherry Blossoms II (Stage Center)*, 2000
    Cibachrome print, mounted on Plexiglas
    32 x 48 in. (81 x 122 cm)
    Courtesy of the artist and Low, Los Angeles, California
    (pp. 12, 24)

19. *Cherry Blossoms III (Stage Right)*, 2000
    Cibachrome print, mounted on Plexiglas
    32 x 48 in. (81 x 122 cm)
    Lawrence Rickels, courtesy Low, Los Angeles, California
    (p. 25)

### ROXY PAINE

20. *Tapioca Slime Painting*, 2001
    Thermoset plastic, lacquer, oil, and aluminum
    36 1/4 x 48 x 9 in. (92 x 122 x 23 cm)
    Courtesy of the artist and Christopher Grimes Gallery, Santa Monica, California
    (pp. 5, 43)

21. *Psilocybe Cubensis Tray*, 1997
    Thermoset, Polymer, lacquer, and oil
    24 1/2 x 17 5/8 x 6 1/2 in. (62 x 45 x 16 cm)
    Lisa and Stuart Ginsberg, courtesy James Cohan Gallery, New York
    (p. 42)

### MICHAEL PIERZYNSKI

22. *Hollywood Reservoir*, 1997
    Painted ceramic and plaster base
    6 x 20 x 12 in. (15 x 51 x 30 cm)
    Courtesy of the artist

23. *Untitled*, 1997
    Painted and underglazed ceramic, and plaster
    8 x 11 x 12 in. (20 x 28 x 30 cm)
    Courtesy of the artist

24. *Cultivating Internal Plastic Infinity*, 1999
    Painted ceramic, gravel, and wood base
    14 x 12 x 7 in. (36 x 30 x 18 cm)
    Courtesy of the artist
    (p. 20)

25. *Untitled*, 2001 (brown)
    Painted ceramic
    4 x 5 x 3 in. (10 x 13 x 8 cm)
    Courtesy of the artist
    (p. 21)

26. *Untitled*, 2001 (dark green)
    4 x 5 x 3 in. (10 x 13 x 8 cm)
    Painted ceramic
    Courtesy of the artist

27. *Untitled*, 2001 (light green)
    4 x 5 x 3 in. (10 x 13 x 8 cm)
    Painted ceramic
    Courtesy of the artist

### MARC QUINN

28. *Garden$^2$*, 2000
    Series of 8 pigment prints
    49 x 31 1/4 in. (124 x 80 cm) each
    Collection of the artist, courtesy eyestorm
    (pp. 1, 32–33)

### MICHELLE SEGRE

29. *Untitled*, 2000
    Beeswax, papier-mâché, acrylic, and metal armature
    43 1/2 x 48 x 34 1/2 in. (110 x 122 x 88 cm)
    Patrick Painter, Santa Monica, California
    (pp. 6, 41)

30. *Opuntia*, 2002
Beeswax, papier-mâché, foam, metal, and paint
65 x 34 x 90 in. (162 x 85 x 225 cm)
(includes base)
Courtesy of the artist and Murray Guy Gallery, New York
(p. 40)

### ALYSON SHOTZ

31. *False Branches #1*, 2001
Lambda print on Fujiflex paper mounted on Sintra
19 x 28 in. (48 x 71 cm)
Courtesy of the artist

32. *False Branches #5*, 2001
Lambda print on Fujiflex paper mounted on Sintra
19 x 28 in. (48 x 71 cm)
Courtesy of the artist
(pp. 16, 38)

33. *Still Life*, 2001
Rubber, steel, tape, Q-tips, casters, and tubing with sound component
9 x 3½ x 3½ ft (274 x 107 x 107 cm)
Courtesy of the artist
(p. 39)

### FRANCES WHITEHEAD

34. *metamohn.dbl ended blk poppy.afm3.ai*, 2001
Epson 9500 digital print on backlit film
36 x 36 in. (91 x 91 cm)
Courtesy of the artist

35. *metamohn.dbl ended blk poppy.afm3.stl*, 2001
Stereolithography and epoxy resin
12 x 6 x 6 in. (30 x 15 x 15 cm)
Courtesy of the artist

36. *metamohn.dbl pop2.afm3.ai*, 2001
Epson 9500 digital print on backlit film
36 x 36 in. (91 x 91 cm)
Courtesy of the artist
(p. 37)

37. *metamohn.dbl pop2.afm3.stl*, 2001
Stereolithography and epoxy resin
12 x 6 x 6 in. (30 x 15 x 15 cm)
Courtesy of the artist
(p. 37)

38. *metamohn.1ptl crkl pop.afm3.ai*, 2002
Epson 9500 digital print on backlit film
36 x 36 in. (91 x 91 cm)
Courtesy of the artist

39. *metamohn.1ptl crkl pop.afm3.stl*, 2002
Stereolithography and epoxy resin
12 x 6 x 6 in. (30 x 15 x 15 cm)
Courtesy of the artist

40. *metamohn.2ptl pop frag.afm3.ai*, 2002
Epson 9500 digital print on backlit film
36 x 36 in. (91 x 91)
Courtesy of the artist
(p. 36)

41. *metamohn.2ptl pop frag.afm3.stl*, 2002
Stereolithography and epoxy resin
12 x 6 x 6 in. (30 x 15 x 15 cm)
Courtesy of the artist
(p. 36)

### CLARA WILLIAMS

42. *Rock*, 2001
Plaster, wood, Styrofoam, and paint
22 x 33 x 26 in. (56 x 84 x 66 cm)
Courtesy Nicole Klagsbrun Gallery, New York
(p. 46)

43. *Scout*, 2001
Plaster, wood, embalmed weasel, and painted plywood column
36 x 31 x 20 in. (91 x 79 x 51 cm)
Courtesy Nicole Klagsbrun Gallery, New York
(p. 47)

# *Artists' Biographies*

**CHRIS ASTLEY** b. 1965, East Lansing, Michigan; B.F.A., University of Michigan, Ann Arbor; currently lives and works in New York. His work has been shown in various group exhibitions in New York, including *4-Ply* (2000, Bronwyn Keenan Gallery) and *Future Perfect* (2001, Silverstein Gallery, New York).

**GREGORY CREWDSON** b. 1962, Brooklyn, New York; B.A., SUNY Purchase, New York, and M.F.A., Yale School of Art, Yale University, New Haven, Connecticut; currently lives and works in New York. He has had solo exhibitions at galleries and museums internationally, including Luhring Augustine Gallery, New York (1995, 2000, 2002), and Cleveland Center for Contemporary Art, Cleveland, Ohio (1997), and has participated in many group exhibitions, such as *La Belle et La Bête* (1995, Musée d'Art Moderne de la Ville de Paris, France), *Making It Real* (1997–99, ICI traveling exhibition), and *Open Ends: Sets and Situations* (2000, Museum of Modern Art, New York).

**JACCI DEN HARTOG** b. 1962, Pella, Iowa; B.F.A., Linfield College, McMinnville, Oregon, and M.F.A., Claremont Graduate School, California; currently lives and works in Los Angeles, California. In addition to solo exhibitions at White Columns, New York (1995), Christopher Grimes Gallery, Santa Monica, California (1996, 1997, 2002), and the San Francisco Art Institute, California (1998), her work has been shown in many group exhibitions, including *Landscape: Outside the Frame* (1999, MIT List Visual Arts Center, Cambridge, Massachusetts), and *Vision Machine* (2000, Musée des Beaux-Arts de Nantes, France).

**ALLAN DESOUZA** b. 1958, Nairobi, Kenya; B.F.A., Bath Academy of Art, Bath, England, and M.F.A., University of California, Los Angeles; currently lives and works in Los Angeles. He has had solo exhibitions at Camerawork, London (1994), Susanne Vielmetter Projects, Los Angeles (2001), and Art in General, New York (2001), and has participated in such group shows as the *Third Havana Biennale* (1989, National Museum of Havana, Cuba), *Out of India* (1997, Queens Museum of Art, Queens, New York), and *Global Address* (2002, Fisher Gallery, University of Southern California, Los Angeles).

**KEITH EDMIER** b. 1967, Chicago, Illinois; California Institute of the Arts, Valencia; currently lives and works in New York. His work has been presented in numerous solo exhibitions at galleries in the United States and abroad, including Friedrich Petzel Gallery, New York (1995, 1998, 1999) and Neugerriemschneider, Berlin, Germany (2000), and in many group exhibitions, including *Gothic* (1997, Institute of Contemporary Art, Boston, Massachusetts), *Age of Influence: Reflections in the Mirror of American Culture* (2000, Museum of Contemporary Art, Chicago, Illinois), and the *2002 Whitney Biennial* (Whitney Museum of American Art, New York).

**IÑIGO MANGLANO-OVALLE** b. 1961, Madrid, Spain; B.F.A., Williams College, Williamstown, Massachusetts, and M.F.A., School of the Art Institute of Chicago; currently lives and works in Chicago. He has had solo exhibitions at the Museum of Contemporary Art, Chicago, Illinois (1993), Wexner Center for the Arts, Columbus, Ohio (2000), and Vienna Secession, Vienna, Austria (2002), and has participated in such group exhibitions as *Searchlight: Consciousness at the Millenium* (1999, California College of Arts and Crafts, San Francisco, California), *2000 Whitney Biennial* (Whitney Museum of American Art, New York), and *010101: Art in Technological Times* (2001, San Francisco Museum of Modern Art).

**JASON MIDDLEBROOK** b. 1966, Jackson, Michigan; B.F.A., University of California, Santa Cruz, and M.F.A., San Francisco Art Institute, California; Whitney Independent Program, 1994–95; currently lives and works in Brooklyn, New York. His solo exhibitions have included *Real Estate* (1996, John Berggruen Gallery, San Francisco) and *Grand Entrance at the Commons* (1999, one-year public installation, Public Art Fund commission at Metro Tech, Brooklyn, New York), and his work has been shown in various group exhibitions, such as *Tiny Shoes* (1994, New Langton Arts, San Francisco, California), *Float* (2000, Sara Meltzer Gallery, New York), and *Pastoral Pop!* (2000, Whitney Museum at Philip Morris, New York).

**NICOLETTA MUNROE** b. 1968, Washington, D.C.; B.F.A., Otis College of Art and Design, Los Angeles, California; currently lives and works in Los Angeles. In addition to solo exhibitions at Low, Los Angeles (2000) and Venetia Kapernekas Fine Arts, New York (2000), her work has been presented in various group exhibitions, including *Trimmings and Scraps* (1997, Gavlak Projects, Los Angeles), *Visual Invasion* (1998, Los Angeles Center for Photographic Studies, Los Angeles), *New Editions* (1998 and 1999, Brooke Alexander Gallery, New York), *Millenium* (1999, TATE, New York), and *Artificial Real* (2000, Low, Los Angeles).

**ROXY PAINE** b. 1966, in New York; Pratt Institute, New York, and College of Santa Fe, New Mexico; currently lives and works in New York. He has had solo exhibitions at Ronald Feldman Fine Arts, New York (1995, 1997, 1999), Christopher Grimes Gallery, Santa Monica, California (2001), and the Rose Art Museum, Brandeis University, Waltham, Massachusetts (2002), among others, and has participated in many group exhibitions, including *Human/Nature* (1995, New Museum of Contemporary Art, New York), *Current/Undercurrent: Working in Brooklyn* (Brooklyn Museum of Art, New York), and *2002 Whitney Biennial* (Whitney Museum of American Art, New York).

**MICHAEL PIERZYNSKI** b. 1957, St. Louis, Missouri; B.F.A., Washington University School of Fine Arts, St. Louis, Missouri; currently lives and works in Los Angeles, California. His work has been shown in solo exhibitions at Casey Kaplan, New York (1997), POST, Los Angeles (1998, 1999), and Christopher Grimes Gallery, Santa Monica, California (2000), among others, and in many group exhibitions, including *Postmarked L.A.* (1995, P.P.O.W., New York), *Wings of Desire* (1998, San Francisco Art Institute, San Francisco), and *Fresh: The Altoids Curiously Strong Collection, 1998–2000* (2001, New Museum of Contemporary Art, New York).

**MARC QUINN** b. 1964, London, England; Cambridge University, Cambridge, England; currently lives and works in London. He has had solo shows at the Jay Jopling/Otis Gallery, London (1988, 1991, 1994, 1995), Gagosian Gallery, New York (1998), Kunstverein Hannover, Germany (1999), Fondazione Prada, Milan (2000), Gronigen Museum, the Netherlands (2000), and Tate Liverpool, England (2002), and has participated in many group exhibitions, including *Real* (1993, Vienna Secession, Vienna, Austria), *Almost Warm & Fuzzy: Childhood and Contemporary Art* (2000–2002, ICI traveling exhibition), and *Iconoclash: Image Wars in Science, Religion, and Art* (2002, Center for Art and Media, Karlsruhe, Germany).

**MICHELLE SEGRE** b. 1965, Tel Aviv, Israel; Tyler School of Art, Rome, and B.F.A. from the Cooper Union School of Art, New York; currently lives and works in New York. In addition to solo exhibitions at Elizabeth Koury Gallery, New York (1993), Susan Inglett, New York (1999), and Murray Guy Gallery, New York (2002), she has participated in such group exhibitions as *Who Chooses Who: 1994 Benefit Gala & Auction* (1994, New Museum of Contemporary Art, New York), *Here: Artist Interventions at the Aldrich Museum* (1998, Ridgefield, Connecticut), and *Almost Warm & Fuzzy: Childhood and Contemporary Art* (2000–2002, ICI traveling exhibition).

**ALYSON SHOTZ** b. 1964, Glendale, Arizona; B.F.A., Rhode Island School of Design, Providence, and M.F.A., University of Seattle, Washington; currently lives and works in Brooklyn, New York. Her work has been shown in solo exhibitions at Susan Inglett, New York (1996, 2002), Lemon Sky Project Space, Los Angeles, California (1997, 2002), and Susquehanna Art Museum, Harrisburg, Pennsylvania (1999), and in various group exhibitions, including *The Best of the Year* (1999, Aldrich Museum, Ridgefield, Connecticut), *Greater New York* (2000, P.S.1 Contemporary Art Center, New York), and *In Medias Res* (2002, Exit Art, New York).

**FRANCES WHITEHEAD** b. 1953, Richmond, Virginia; B.F.A., East Carolina University, Greenville, North Carolina, and M.F.A., Northern Illinois University, DeKalb; currently lives and works in Chicago, Illinois. Her work has been shown in solo exhibitions at Laumeier Sculpture Park, St. Louis, Missouri (1996) and Northern Illinois University Gallery, Chicago (2000), among others, and in many group exhibitions, including *Recent Acquisitions* (1987, Museum of Contemporary Art, Chicago, Illinois), *The Return of the Exquisite Corpse* (1993, Drawing Center, New York), and *Digital Prints: Prints Biennial 2001* (Brooklyn Museum of Art, New York).

**CLARA WILLIAMS** b. 1972, Nashville, Tennessee; B.F.A., School of Visual Arts, New York; currently lives and works in New Haven, Connecticut. In addition to solo exhibitions at Cheekwood Museum of Art, Nashville, Tennessee (2000) and Nicole Klagsbrun Gallery, New York (2000, 2002), her work has been shown in group exhibitions such as *Small World: Dioramas in Contemporary Art* (2000, Museum of Contemporary Art, San Diego, California), *Greater New York* (2000, P.S.1 Contemporary Art Center, New York), and *Beyond City Limits* (2001, Socrates Sculpture Park, Long Island City, New York).

**PHOTO CREDITS**

Ron Amstutz, p. 40; Chris Astley, pp. 3, 5, 28–29; Allan de Souza, pp. 4, 30–31; Luhring Augustine Gallery, New York, pp. 26–27; Margaret Fox, p. 42; Christopher Grimes Gallery, Santa Monica, California, pp. 2, 5, 34–35, 43; Scott Lindgren, p. 6, 41; Low, Los Angeles, California, pp. 12, 24–25; Bill Orcutt, pp. 44–45; Friedrich Petzel Gallery, pp. 22–23; Michael Pierzynski, pp. 20–21; Max Protetch Gallery, New York, p. 19; Leslee and David Rogath/ Martin Lawrence Galleries, pp. 1, 32–33; Alyson Shotz, pp. 16, 38–39; Frances Whitehead, pp. 36–37; Clara Williams, pp. 46–47